MASTERING
MEAL
PREP

EASY RECIPES AND TIME-SAVING TIPS TO PREPARE A WEEK OF
DELICIOUS MAKE-AHEAD MEALS IN JUST ONE HOUR

PAMELA ELLGEN

Ulysses Press

Published in the United States by:
ULYSSES PRESS
P.O. Box 3440
Berkeley, CA 94703
www.ulyssespress.com

ISBN: 978-1-61243-841-2
Library of Congress Control Number: 2018944074

Printed in Canada by Marquis Book Printing
10 9 8 7 6 5 4 3 2 1

Acquisitions editor: Bridget Thoreson
Managing editor: Claire Chun
Editor: Renee Rutledge
Proofreader: Shayna Keyles
Front cover design: Rebecca Lown
Interior design and production: Jake Flaherty

Distributed by Publishers Group West

■ ■ ■ ■ ■
CONTENTS

WEEK 1: WINNER, WINNER CHICKEN DINNER 8

WEEK 2: BEEF, IT'S WHAT'S FOR DINNER 24

INTRODUCTION

When I began this project, the idea of meal preparation held many different meanings to me. It meant the soups and casseroles of the 1980s, prepared once a month using canned ingredients and then frozen into bricks until ready to serve. It meant the endless stacked containers of chicken breast, brown rice, and broccoli designed for a bodybuilder before competition. And it meant the meal-in-a-box delivery services such as HelloFresh or Blue Apron that offered all the ingredients you needed to make a complete meal.

The most captivating concept of meal preparation came to me from chef and food writer Tamar Adler in her book *An Everlasting Meal*. In it, she describes one meal tumbling effortlessly into the next. One day you make a big pot of beans. The next day it becomes a savory *ribollita*, an Italian bread and bean soup. The next day, the beans become a thick puree topped with blanched greens. I find this concept so appealing, and it is one that I have tried to adopt in my kitchen and in this book.

I believe cooking should not be a huge chore, and meal preparation shouldn't consume an entire weekend. *Mastering Meal Prep* acts as a guidebook of sorts for creating a few foundation recipes that will carry you through the week. You can follow the suggested menu for using those recipes, called "Main Meals" throughout, or you can do as I most often do and just wing it. With a few foods prepped in advance, you will always be well fed.

■ ■ ■ ■
MEAL PREP ESSENTIALS

In this book, meal preparation takes a different approach from many popular guides on the topic. My goal is for meal prep to make your life less complicated, make cooking more fun, and make meals that are both healthy and delicious!

MEAL-PREPPING BASICS

I define "meal prep" as planning a menu, preparing ingredients, and cooking strategically to yield simple, healthy, and delicious food that's ready to enjoy straight from the refrigerator or with only a few minutes of active cooking time or up to an hour in the oven.

Each chapter in *Mastering Meal Prep* has a theme and a (super-cheesy) title. Each one is designed to stand alone and offers a unique menu, shopping list, recipes, and prep day schedule for one week. This means you don't have to flip back and forth between chapters to find the essential recipes.

Each chapter also features a handful of foundation recipes. These typically consist of one or two proteins, along with a starch, vegetables, and sauces. The foundation recipes can be prepared within a one-hour time frame and serve as the building blocks for meals throughout the week. Some weeks also include a few additional prep day tasks, such as chopping vegetables or assembling a casserole. You can follow the suggested menus I offer for using those ingredients, or you can come up with your own combinations.

All of the main meal recipes combined yield at least 20 servings, which provide lunch and dinner for two people for five days. It's up to you when you want to enjoy each meal, and many are freezer-friendly, so you can save any unused portions for later if you go out to eat or make other plans.

The meal prep day can happen any day of the week, but I find it works best on the last day of my weekend, which is Sunday. That's when I prepare all of the foundation recipes. I then enjoy the first main meal of the week that night.

THE RECIPES

The recipes in this book are designed to maximize your time so that you can cook one ingredient and use it several different ways. Most weeks feature one large portion of protein that is strategically deployed to a few different meals. For example, a whole roast chicken is served as pulled chicken tacos and in a hearty chicken pot pie. Starches and cooked vegetables are used similarly, artfully filling multiple recipes.

Each recipe includes the cooking time required for that day. The additional cooking time will have been completed on the meal prep day. For example, if a recipe calls for cooked brown rice, the time required to cook it is not included in the recipe. Instead, it is included in the one hour of advanced preparation. Make sure to read each chapter thoroughly before you shop and get started prepping. That way you won't be tethered to the cookbook every second of the preparation.

SERVING SIZES

What is a portion size? For one person, 400 calories might be a meal. For another, that is a snack. In my family, we're very active and frequently run, surf, practice yoga, and lift weights. Hence, I eat around 600 calories at lunch and dinner, and my husband, Rich, eats even more.

But, everyone's needs are different. I considered this carefully when planning the portion sizes in this book and opted for smaller portion sizes that can easily be multiplied for athletes and those with very active lifestyles.

Recipes in this book yield four or more servings of approximately 350 to 600 calories each for lunches and dinners and about 200 to 300 in the breakfast chapter. Of course, you will want to tailor each recipe to meet your needs. If that's not enough food—or if you need to prepare meals for more people—simply double the recipe. If the recipes offer more food than you need, you can cut the recipe in half, or better yet, store the leftovers. I provide storage tips for any recipe that can easily be frozen and defrosted.

Also, meat shrinks by about 25 percent during cooking. Hence, the raw weight will be roughly 4 ounces per serving of lean protein but will yield about 3 ounces per portion (occasionally less in some recipes with multiple sources of protein). For example, in Shredded Chicken Tacos with Pickled Onions (page 22), the recipe calls for 14 ounces of shredded cooked chicken. If you do not have a scale, simply estimate the portion size using a deck of cards as a visual cue for one portion. Of course, many pieces of meat do not lend themselves well to being smooshed into a measuring cup, so use a simple kitchen scale if you have one.

DIETARY RESTRICTIONS

Look for these icons that identify if a recipe is free from gluten, dairy, eggs, and nuts. Also noted are recipes that are vegan or vegetarian.

Gluten Free   Dairy Free   Egg Free   Nut Free   Vegan   Vegetarian

However, all recipes are easily adaptable to a gluten-free or dairy-free diet and I've recommended substitutions in the ingredient list where appropriate.

In addition, I've provided notes to make recipes gluten free, dairy free, egg free, nut free, and plant based, when possible.

ESSENTIAL EQUIPMENT

I am a minimalist when it comes to equipment. For years, I rolled out my pie crusts without a rolling pin, opting for a pint glass instead (I don't recommend that!). So, when it comes to equipment, I only ask you to buy the things you really can't live without.

Rimmed baking sheet. Also known as a half sheet pan, the rimmed baking sheet will be used to cook many of the foundation recipes in this book. Invest in one or two sturdy pans and the largest size that will fit in your oven. You're going to need all of that real estate to get the most out of your prep work.

Medium and large stock pot. I used two 4-quart pots and occasionally one 8-quart pot while preparing the recipes in this book. Whenever food was being cooked on the stovetop, I used no more than three pots or pans at a time because it can get crowded quickly, especially when you're using large skillets. Invest in heavy-bottom pots with glass lids.

Small and large oven-safe skillets. I used one 8-inch skillet, one 16-inch skillet, and one 14-inch cast iron pan for preparing the recipes in this book. All of my skillets are oven-safe, meaning I can transfer them from the stovetop to the oven without damaging the pan. That is not an essential feature in all recipes, but it's nice to have the flexibility to use it if you need to.

Grill or grill pan. I used a charcoal grill to prepare the grilled recipes in this book. A gas grill or stovetop grill pan will work just as well.

Casserole dishes. You will need a few glass or ceramic baking dishes. Not only are these used for cooking, but they're also used for storing food in the refrigerator after prep and before baking. I use one 8 x 10-inch glass baking dish, one 9-inch deep-dish pie plate, and one 2-quart casserole dish. The pie plate accommodates a prepared pie crust for chicken pot pie, for example. The casserole dish can be any shape. Individual ceramic ramekins are also a fun thing to have around, but they're not essential.

Blender. A countertop blender or immersion blender is helpful in preparing many of the recipes in this book. It does not need to be an expensive model; the consumer variety is just fine for these purposes.

Food processor. To save time, I prepped many ingredients in a food processor. Unless you have deft knife skills, you'll appreciate its safe and quick operation. I like the grating and slicing attachments over the s-blade because they produce uniform slices.

Measuring devices. A set of liquid and dry measuring cups and a set of measuring spoons are essential to prepare the recipes in this book. Measuring devices are especially important if you're counting macros. I also highly recommend investing in a kitchen scale. I use it often for counting macros and sometimes in baking.

Food-storage containers. The options are limitless here, and clever marketing suggests so many cute options. So, have fun if you like. But really, all you need are a few glass dishes with plastic, rubber, or silicon lids. I recommend glass over plastic because it is safer for using in the microwave and contains none of the harmful chemicals present in plastic and even stainless steel (especially if the product is manufactured in China).

Food-labeling supplies. Use a permanent marker to write on disposable containers (such as zip-top plastic bags) or on masking tape for labeling food. Write the name of the food, the volume, what it will be used for (if applicable), and the date. For example: Sliced onions, 1 cup, for shepherd's pie, 2/28.

INGREDIENTS

Is there anything worse than accumulating numerous bottles of condiments or jars of spices you'll never use again? I still have half a liter of fish sauce in my refrigerator that I haven't touched in a year. What a waste!

In this book, I use spices judiciously and repeat the same spices, vinegars, and oils throughout, so even if some doesn't get used in one week, you'll be sure to use it in another week down the road. Here are the ingredients you will see throughout this book. Some may be new or unfamiliar. Others are probably in your pantry already.

Cumin: A pungent spice that is prevalent in Latin and Middle Eastern cooking.

Smoked paprika: Smoky, slightly sweet, barely spicy chile powder.

Crushed red pepper: Dried red chilies that are excellent for adding heat to recipes.

Sambal: A spicy chile paste good for spicing up cooked food or adding to salad dressings, stir fries, and sauces.

Toasted sesame oil: Adds a lot of flavor in a small amount.

Red wine vinegar: Flavorful and good for salad dressings.

Apple cider vinegar: Slightly sweeter, good for pickles and salad dressings.

Low-sodium soy sauce: Choose gluten-free soy sauce if you follow a gluten-free diet.

Maple syrup or brown sugar: Can be used interchangeably in most recipes. Use sparingly.

KEEP WHAT YOU LOVE

If you're like most people, including me, you buy a cookbook, bookmark five to ten recipes you want to try, eventually get around to making three or four of them, and then shelve the book. Only a few books on my shelf offer recipes that are worth making again and again. But the underutilized books are never wasted. From them, I glean new techniques, learn about new ingredients, and consider flavor combinations I had never thought of before. Sometimes even just a photo inspires me to make something similar with the ingredients I have on hand.

In writing this book, I had to acknowledge that you probably aren't going to cook through each and every week exactly as it's written. Maybe you're just not a fan of certain ingredients. Maybe you have company coming to town and decide to serve the entire roast chicken in one meal. Maybe you're mostly vegetarian and just want the meat-free options. Whatever your approach, I want this book to bring value to your kitchen. I hope you learn more about batch cooking, develop strategies that streamline your cooking process, and introduce many new healthy and delicious recipes into your menu!

COMMON CONVERSIONS

1 gallon = 4 quarts = 8 pints = 16 cups = 128 fluid ounces = 3.8 liters
1 quart = 2 pints = 4 cups = 32 ounces = .95 liter
1 pint = 2 cups = 16 ounces = 480 ml
1 cup = 8 ounces = 240 ml
¼ cup = 4 tablespoons = 12 teaspoons = 2 ounces = 60 ml
1 tablespoon = 3 teaspoons = ½ fluid ounce = 15 ml

TEMPERATURE CONVERSIONS

Fahrenheit (°F)	Celsius (°C)
145°F	63°C
155°C	68°C
165°C	74°C
350°F	175°C
375°F	190°C
400°F	200°C
425°F	220°C

WEIGHT CONVERSIONS

US	Metric
½ ounce	15 grams
1 ounce	30 grams
¼ pound	115 grams
⅓ pound	150 grams
¾ pound	350 grams
1 pound	450 grams

WEEK 1

■ ■ ■ ■

WINNER, WINNER CHICKEN DINNER

You can do so much with a whole roasted chicken, and this chapter offers a few options. Roasting the chicken is one of the foundation recipes you'll make on prep day. Although it's really an easy, hands-off process once the bird goes in the oven, you can also just purchase a rotisserie chicken at the grocery store and skip that step. Remember, there are no rules— this is your book, make it work for you! If you have leftovers, check out the freezer-friendly tips throughout.

FOUNDATION RECIPES

Roasted Chicken

Herb Roasted Potatoes

Chicken Stock

Steamed Jasmine Rice

Pickled Red Onion

Lemon Herb Vinaigrette

Additional Prep Day Tasks

Assemble Chicken Pot Pie

MAIN MEALS

Roasted Chicken and Herb Roasted Potatoes with Green Salad

"Spicy Tuna Roll" Bowl

Chicken Pot Pie

Shredded Chicken Tacos with Pickled Onions

Tofu Fried Rice

WEEK 1 SHOPPING LIST

PANTRY STAPLES

- ☐ Extra-virgin olive oil
- ☐ Canola oil
- ☐ Apple cider vinegar
- ☐ Red wine vinegar

- ☐ 1 (8-ounce) bottle low-sodium soy sauce
- ☐ White sugar
- ☐ Brown sugar

- ☐ All-purpose flour or gluten-free flour blend
- ☐ Crushed red pepper
- ☐ Sea salt
- ☐ Freshly ground pepper

MEAT, POULTRY, AND FISH

- ☐ 1 whole (5-pound) chicken
- ☐ 1 pound frozen ahi tuna

- ☐ 1 (8-ounce) package smoked tofu or cooked ham

DAIRY AND EGGS

- ☐ 4 eggs

FROZEN

☐ 1 (16-ounce) bag frozen peas and carrots blend

☐ 1 (9-inch) frozen pie crust

DELI

☐ 1 (16-ounce) container pico de gallo, or prepare Pico de Gallo (page 65)

PACKAGED AND BULK FOODS

☐ 1 package corn tortillas, at least 12 count

☐ 1 (2-pound) bag jasmine rice

CANNED GOODS

☐ 1 (4-ounce) can chipotle in adobo sauce

☐ 1 (6-ounce) can tomato paste

☐ 1 (9-ounce) bottle sriracha

☐ 1 (8-ounce) jar mayonnaise

PRODUCE

☐ 3 pounds Yukon Gold potatoes

☐ 1 (8-ounce) bag shredded cabbage

☐ 1 (8-ounce) bag washed salad greens

☐ 1 pint grape tomatoes

☐ 1 medium yellow onion

☐ 1 small red onion

☐ 2 semi-ripe avocados

☐ 1 bunch scallions

☐ 1 bunch radishes

☐ 2 limes

☐ 1 bunch cilantro

☐ 1 package fresh thyme, rosemary, or parsley

☐ 1 lemon

☐ 1 small knob ginger

☐ 1 shallot

☐ 1 head garlic

SAVVY SHORTCUTS

- Buy a rotisserie chicken.
- Buy boxed chicken stock.
- Buy precooked, frozen jasmine rice.
- Buy bottled lemon herb salad dressing.

Roasted Chicken

Master this roasted chicken and you will master one of the most essential elements of meal prepping. This is the basic version that is used in the recipes this week but see the following page for several different flavor combinations you can use in your own menu to really transform the bird and liven up your leftovers.

YIELD: 16 (3-ounce) servings (varies depending on initial size of bird) | PREP TIME: 5 minutes | COOK TIME: 40 minutes

1 (5-pound) chicken, preferably organic, free range

2 tablespoons canola oil

sea salt

freshly ground pepper

1. Preheat the oven to 400°F.

2. Using a serrated knife or sharp kitchen shears, cut down one side of the chicken backbone, slicing through the ribs. Carefully cut down the other side to remove the backbone.

3. Place the chicken onto a rimmed baking sheet with the cut side down, spreading out the legs. Press down between the breasts to flatten the chicken. Pat it dry with paper towels.

4. Rub the chicken with the oil. Season with salt and pepper on both sides.

5. Bake for 10 minutes, then reduce the heat to 350°F.

6. Bake for another 30 minutes, or until the chicken is cooked through and reaches an internal temperature of 155°F. It will continue cooking after it comes out of the oven and reach an internal temperature of 165°F. Allow to rest for 10 minutes before slicing.

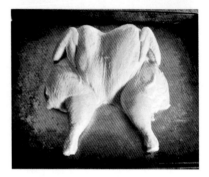

7. To serve, slice light or dark meat from the chicken and place about 3 ounces of meat onto each plate or container.

NUTRITION PER SERVING: 146 calories, fat 8g, protein 18g, carbohydrate 0g, fiber 0g

Freezer Friendly: Cool individual chicken pieces (with or without the bone), then place individual portions into zip-top plastic bags. Remove as much air as you can from the bags before sealing. Mark the bags, and then refrigerate.

Southwestern salsa: garlic powder, onion powder, smoked paprika, ground cumin

East Indian curry: turmeric, ground coriander, ground ginger, ground cumin

Jamaican jerk: allspice, ground cumin, ground nutmeg, ground cloves, ground cayenne

Italian herb: dried oregano, dried thyme, dried parsley, garlic powder

BBQ: onion powder, garlic powder, smoked paprika, dry mustard powder, brown sugar

Herb Roasted Potatoes

These roasted potatoes add depth to Chicken Pot Pie (page 21) and provide a tasty side dish for the first main meal of the week. They're also delicious over salad.

YIELD: 12 (1-cup) servings | PREP TIME: 5 minutes | COOK TIME: 25 to 30 minutes

1. Preheat the oven to 400°F.

2. Spread the potatoes on a sheet pan. Drizzle with oil and season with the herbs, salt, and pepper. Toss to coat the potatoes in the herbs and oil.

3. Bake for 25 to 30 minutes until the potatoes are golden brown and crisp.

NUTRITION PER SERVING: 101 calories, fat 2g, protein 2g, carbohydrate 18g, fiber 3g

3 pounds Yukon Gold potatoes, larger ones halved

2 tablespoons canola oil

¼ cup minced fresh herbs, such as rosemary, parsley, and thyme

sea salt

freshly ground pepper

Chicken Stock

The difference between broth and stock is often overstated, but generally speaking, stock is made from the bones, and broth is made from meat and possibly bones and vegetables. This recipe uses bones with the barest amount of skin and meat and transforms what otherwise might have been fit for the bin into a flavorful chicken stock. It will make your Chicken Pot Pie and Shredded Chicken Tacos delectable, along with soups, stews, risotto, and more.

YIELD: 4 (1-cup) servings | PREP TIME: 5 minutes | COOK TIME: 45 minutes

chicken backbone and other chicken bones

8 cups water

sea salt

1. Place the chicken backbone and any other chicken bones (neck, etc.) that were inside the chicken into a stock pot and cover with the water. Season with salt and bring to a boil. Reduce the heat to a simmer and cook for 45 minutes.

2. Strain the stock, discarding the bones. Place into a heat-proof container. Store the broth in the refrigerator for up to 5 days.

NUTRITION PER SERVING: 10 calories, fat 1g, protein 1g, carbohydrate 0g, fiber 0g

Freezer Friendly: There are two options for making this freezer friendly. The first is to store leftover chicken bones in a large, sealed container in the freezer until you have a few pounds of bones and then make a large pot of stock. The second option is to make the recipe as directed above and then freeze the broth in plastic containers (glass has a tendency to break in the freezer unless carefully handled), and freeze for up to 6 months until you're ready to defrost and use in a recipe.

Steamed Jasmine Rice

Jasmine rice has a pleasant floral aroma and buttery flavor that brings a lot to the dishes that call for it later in the week. You can also use long-grain white rice or basmati rice if that's what you have.

YIELD: 16 (½-cup) servings | PREP TIME: 5 minutes | COOK TIME: 15 minutes

Place water and sea salt in a large pot and bring to a simmer. Add the jasmine rice, stir, cover, and reduce the heat to low. Cook for 15 minutes, or until the rice is tender.

5½ cups water

1 teaspoon sea salt

3 cups jasmine rice

NUTRITION PER SERVING: 102 calories, fat 0g, protein 2g, carbohydrate 22g, fiber 0g

Lemon Herb Vinaigrette

After making my own salad dressings for several years, I can't imagine going back to the bottled stuff. Nevertheless, there's something to be said for the convenience of bottled dressings. That's why I like to make a simple vinaigrette at the beginning of each week. It yields 1 cup of dressing, which will dress 8 portions of salad.

YIELD: 1 cup, or 8 (2-tablespoon) servings | PREP TIME: 5 minutes | COOK TIME: 0 minutes

1. Combine the vinegar, lemon juice, olive oil, thyme, shallot, sugar, and salt in a jar.

2. Seal tightly with a lid and shake vigorously to combine. Store in the refrigerator for up to 5 days.

¼ cup red wine vinegar

2 tablespoons fresh lemon juice

½ cup extra-virgin olive oil

1 teaspoon minced fresh thyme

1 shallot, minced

1 teaspoon white sugar (maple syrup or honey are okay)

½ teaspoon sea salt

NUTRITION PER SERVING: 123 calories, fat 14g, protein 0g, carbohydrate 1g, fiber 0g

Pickled Red Onion

Many foods need just a touch of acidity to liven up their flavors, and pickled onions are a pretty tasty way to bring it. Warning, these are totally addicting.

YIELD: ½ pint (4 servings) | PREP TIME: 5 minutes | COOK TIME: 1 minute

1. Place the sliced onion in a clean ½-pint glass jar.

2. Combine the vinegar, water, salt, and sugar in a heat-proof dish. Microwave for 1 minute. Stir to dissolve the sugar and salt.

3. When they have completely dissolved, pour the liquid over the onions. Cover and refrigerate until ready to serve.

NUTRITION PER SERVING: 11 calories, fat 0g, protein 0g, carbohydrate 3g, fiber 0g

½ red onion, thinly sliced

1/3 cup apple cider vinegar

¼ cup water

1½ teaspoons sea salt

1½ teaspoons sugar

Roasted Chicken and Herbed Potatoes

I like to serve this dish on the same day that meal prepping takes place so that it is hot and fresh from the oven. Serve with the Green Salad with Lemon Herb Vinaigrette for a complete meal.

YIELD: **4** servings | PREP TIME: **5** minutes | COOK TIME: **40** minutes

Divide the chicken and potatoes between serving plates.

NUTRITION PER SERVING: 348 calories, fat 12g, protein 22g, carbohydrate 36g, fiber 6g

Freezer Friendly: Cool individual chicken pieces (with or without the bone), then place them into usable portions into a zip-top plastic bag. Remove as much air as you can from the bag before sealing. Mark the bag, and then freeze.

12 to 16 ounces Roasted Chicken (page 11), cooked light and dark meat with skin

6 cups Herb Roasted Potatoes (page 13)

Green Salad with Lemon Herb Vinaigrette

This side salad is a nice accompaniment to the Roasted Chicken and Herbed Potatoes (above) or can be served alongside the Chicken Pot Pie (page 21).

YIELD: **4** servings | PREP TIME: **5** minutes | COOK TIME: **0** minutes

Just before serving, combine all of the ingredients in a large mixing bowl. Toss gently to mix. Divide between serving plates.

NUTRITION PER SERVING: 139 calories, fat 14g, protein 1g, carbohydrate 4g, fiber 1g

8 ounces salad greens (about 6 cups)

1 cup halved grape tomatoes

2 to 4 radishes, julienned

½ cup Lemon Herb Vinaigrette (page 15)

"Spicy Tuna Roll" Bowl

When Rich and I were dating, we frequented an Asian fusion restaurant that served an amazing spicy tuna roll during happy hour. This deconstructed tuna roll has all of the intoxicating flavors of the original, with minimal effort. No sushi mat required. Also, be prepared to meet your favorite new condiment—sriracha aioli.

YIELD: **4 servings** | PREP TIME: **10 minutes** | COOK TIME: **3 minutes**

1. Whisk the sriracha aioli together until combined.

2. Warm the rice in the microwave in a covered container with 1 to 2 tablespoons of water for 1 to 2 minutes, or until heated through.

3. Pat the tuna steaks dry with paper towels. Rub the tuna with the oil and season on both sides with salt and pepper.

4. Heat a large skillet over medium-high heat until very hot. Sear the tuna for 90 seconds on each side for medium-rare. Transfer to a cutting board and slice on a bias into ½-inch-thick pieces.

5. To serve, divide the cooked rice between serving bowls. Top with the cooked tuna, avocado, radish slices, and scallion. Drizzle with 1½ tablespoons of the sriracha aioli and garnish with a lime wedge.

NUTRITION PER SERVING: 478 calories, fat 18g, protein 30g, carbohydrate 52g, fiber 2g

For the sriracha aioli:

¼ cup real mayonnaise

1½ tablespoons sriracha

2 teaspoons low-sodium, gluten-free soy sauce

For the bowl:

4 cups cooked Jasmine Rice (page 15)

16 ounces ahi tuna

2 teaspoons canola oil

1 avocado, thinly sliced

4 radishes, thinly sliced

1 scallion, thinly sliced on a bias

1 lime, quartered

sea salt

freshly ground pepper

Chicken Pot Pie

A passable chicken pot pie is easy to put together, but for true comfort food, use roasted chicken and potatoes and homemade chicken broth. Even better, pour in any pan drippings remaining from the roasting pan. They bring complexity and depth to the dish, making it taste as if it took hours to prepare. Complete steps 1 through 5 on your weekend prep day.

YIELD: 4 servings | PREP TIME: 15 minutes (including stovetop cooking) | COOK TIME: 30 to 45 minutes

1. Preheat the oven to 400°F.

2. Heat a large skillet over medium heat. Add canola oil. Cook the onions and minced thyme until they begin to soften, about 5 minutes.

3. Add the flour. Cook for 1 minute, or until the flour is dissolved. Add the chicken stock and simmer until the sauce is thickened, about 1 minute.

4. Stir in the frozen peas and carrots, diced roasted potatoes, and chicken meat. Season to taste with salt and pepper.

5. Transfer the mixture to a 9-inch pie dish.

6. Top with the prepared pie crust. Bake for 30 minutes if the filling is still warm or 45 minutes if chilled.

NUTRITION PER SERVING: 501 calories, fat 26g, protein 22g, carbohydrate 44g, fiber 6g

Freezer Friendly: Freeze the filling in a pie dish covered tightly with plastic wrap. To bake, allow to defrost for 2 days in the refrigerator, top with the prepared pie crust, and bake as instructed.

Make Plant Based: Swap the chicken for one 10-ounce package Gardein Chick'n Scallopini, diced. Use vegetable broth in place of chicken stock.

1 tablespoon canola oil

1 yellow onion, diced

1 teaspoon minced fresh thyme

2 tablespoons all-purpose flour or gluten-free flour blend

1 cup Chicken Stock (page 14)

1½ cups frozen peas and carrots

2 cups diced Herb Roasted Potatoes (page 13)

2 cups (10 ounces) shredded Roasted Chicken (page 11)

1 (9-inch) prepared pie crust (use gluten-free if needed)

sea salt

freshly ground pepper

Shredded Chicken Tacos with Pickled Onions

Light and dark chicken meat are simmered in a rich combination of chipotle in adobo sauce, tomato paste, chicken broth, brown sugar, and a splash of vinegar.

YIELD: 4 servings | PREP TIME: 5 minutes | COOK TIME: 5 minutes

2 tablespoons tomato paste

1 tablespoon minced chipotle in adobo sauce

½ cup Chicken Stock (page 14)

1 tablespoon apple cider vinegar

1 tablespoon brown sugar

¼ teaspoon sea salt

2¾ cups (14 ounces) shredded Roasted Chicken (page 11)

12 corn tortillas

1½ cups pico de gallo salsa

1 avocado, thinly sliced

1 cup Pickled Red Onion (page 16)

1½ cups shredded cabbage

1. Mix the tomato paste, chipotle, stock, vinegar, brown sugar, and salt along with the shredded cooked chicken in a small skillet over medium-low heat. Cover and cook until heated through.

2. To serve, warm the corn tortillas individually for about 12 seconds each in the microwave.

3. Divide the shredded Roasted Chicken between the warmed corn tortillas. Top with pico de gallo, avocado, pickled red onion, and cabbage.

NUTRITION PER SERVING: 426 calories, fat 10g, protein 37g, carbohydrate 48g, fiber 8g

Tofu Fried Rice

The beauty of fried rice is that it works best with day-old (or even a few days old) rice because the grains of rice become distinct and dries out slightly, allowing them to absorb all of the yummy ginger and soy sauce you add to the dish. If you prep the other ingredients ahead of time, you'll have dinner ready in a flash!

YIELD: **4 servings** | PREP TIME: **5 minutes** | COOK TIME: **7 minutes**

1. Heat a large skillet over medium-high heat. When it is hot, add 1 tablespoon of the oil and tilt to coat the pan. Allow the oil to warm for at least 10 seconds.

2. Pour the eggs into the pan and allow to cook until nearly set, about 2 minutes. Using a spatula, carefully flip the omelet. It's okay if it breaks a little. Cook on the second side for about 30 seconds, or until just cooked through. Fold the omelet into quarters and slide onto a cutting board.

3. Return the skillet to the heat, reducing it to medium. Add the remaining tablespoon of oil, ginger, garlic, and crushed red pepper to the pan. Cook for about 15 seconds, or just until fragrant.

4. Add the rice and tofu or ham. Cook for about 3 minutes.

5. Thinly slice the omelet into ribbons.

6. Add the sliced omelet, defrosted peas and carrots, soy sauce, and green onions to the pan. Cook for another minute, or until just heated through.

7. Garnish with fresh cilantro.

NUTRITION PER SERVING: 416 calories, fat 15g, protein 18g, carbohydrate 53g, fiber 3g

2 tablespoons canola oil

4 eggs, whisked

1 tablespoon minced ginger

1 tablespoon minced garlic

pinch crushed red pepper

4 cups Steamed Jasmine Rice (page 15)

8 ounces smoked tofu or ham, diced

1½ cups frozen peas and carrots, defrosted under running water

3 tablespoons low-sodium and/or gluten-free soy sauce

2 green onions, thinly sliced on a bias

¼ cup minced fresh cilantro

WEEK 2

■ ■ ■ ■ ■

BEEF, IT'S WHAT'S FOR DINNER

The primary protein this week is flank steak, which is taken from the underside of the cow and is often used in place of skirt steak. Often used in Asian cooking, flank steak should be cut across the grain to make it less fibrous. The primary cooking techniques utilized this week are stovetop boiling, blanching, and steaming. These techniques vary only slightly, and they are appropriate for a wide array of ingredients, including rice, vegetables, eggs, and potatoes. Even better, the water can be reused as you move from one ingredient to the next. Two sauces round out the week, including salsa verde and a tangy hoisin stir-fry sauce.

FOUNDATION RECIPES	MAIN MEALS
Rosemary Garlic Grilled Flank Steak	Hoisin Beef and Green Bean Stir-Fry
Perfectly Cooked Brown Rice	Bibimbap
Blanched Green Beans	Sautéed Tomato Rice Pilaf with Salsa Verde Salmon
Boiled Potatoes	
Soft-Boiled Eggs	Flank Steak Tacos
Salsa Verde	Vegetarian Niçoise Salad
Hoisin Stir-Fry Sauce	

WEEK 2 SHOPPING LIST

PANTRY STAPLES

- ☐ Extra-virgin olive oil
- ☐ Canola oil
- ☐ Toasted sesame oil
- ☐ Crushed red pepper
- ☐ White wine vinegar
- ☐ Low-sodium soy sauce
- ☐ Dijon mustard
- ☐ Maple syrup or brown sugar
- ☐ Sea salt
- ☐ Freshly ground black pepper

MEAT, POULTRY, AND FISH

- ☐ 3½ pounds flank steak or skirt steak
- ☐ 1 pound salmon

DAIRY AND EGGS

- ☐ 1 dozen large eggs
- ☐ 1 (4-ounce) package queso fresco

DELI

- ☐ 1 (8-ounce) jar kimchi, optional

PACKAGED AND BULK FOODS

- ☐ 1 package corn tortillas (minimum 12 count)
- ☐ 1 pound long-grain brown rice

CANNED GOODS

- ☐ 1 (8-ounce) jar Niçoise olives or another black olive
- ☐ 1 (8-ounce) jar hoisin sauce

PRODUCE

- ☐ 1 head garlic
- ☐ 1 shallot
- ☐ 1 (2-inch) piece fresh ginger
- ☐ 1 bunch fresh rosemary
- ☐ 1 bunch fresh cilantro
- ☐ 1 jalapeno pepper
- ☐ 1 pound Yukon Gold potatoes
- ☐ 2 pints grape or cherry tomatoes
- ☐ 2 pounds green beans
- ☐ 3 limes
- ☐ 1 bunch green onions
- ☐ 1 pound or 1 (16-ounce) bag fresh spinach
- ☐ 1 (10-ounce) bag mixed baby lettuce
- ☐ 1 (10-ounce) bag shredded cabbage
- ☐ 1 carrot
- ☐ 1 avocado

Rosemary Garlic Grilled Flank Steak

This delicious grilled flank steak is just as flavorful straight off the grill as it is incorporated into several of this week's meals. Rosemary, garlic, soy sauce, and maple syrup infuse the steak with flavor that's versatile enough to be at home in Flank Steak Tacos or Hoisin Beef and Green Bean Stir-Fry. If you prefer not to light a propane or charcoal grill, heat a large grill pan or a cast iron skillet on the stovetop instead.

YIELD: 3½ pounds steak or 14 (3-ounce) servings | PREP TIME: 5 minutes, plus 45 minutes inactive time | COOK TIME: 8 minutes

1. Combine the garlic, rosemary, pepper, salt, soy sauce, maple syrup, and canola oil in a large glass baking dish. Add the flank steak and turn to coat. Set aside to marinate for about 45 minutes (or up to 8 hours in the refrigerator).

2. Preheat a grill to medium-high heat. Remove the steak from the marinade. Grill the steak for 2 minutes on each side for medium-rare, or to your desired level of doneness.

NUTRITION PER SERVING: 188 calories, fat 9g, protein 24g, carbohydrate 1g, fiber 0g

Freezer Friendly: Divide the cooked steak into desired portion sizes and place into zip-top bags. Remove all excess air from the bags and seal. Label and store for up to 1 month.

Tip: Meat loses about 25 percent of its weight during cooking, so the 56 ounces (3½ pounds) of raw meat used for this recipe will become 42 ounces (2⅗ pounds).

1 tablespoon minced garlic

1 tablespoon minced fresh rosemary

1 tablespoon freshly ground pepper

1 teaspoon sea salt

½ cup low-sodium and/ or gluten-free soy sauce

¼ cup maple syrup or brown sugar

¼ cup canola oil

3½ pounds flank steak

Perfectly Cooked Brown Rice

If you're skittish about brown rice because it often turns to mush, follow these simple instructions for perfectly cooked brown rice every time. The trick is to boil the rice in several times the amount of water you might normally use—as you do for pasta—and then drain it and return it to the pot to steam. This yields tender rice with each grain distinct. Bonus, it may also wash away some impurities found in commercially available rice.

YIELD: 7 to 8 cups cooked brown rice, or 14 to 16 (½-cup) servings | PREP TIME: 5 minutes | COOK TIME: 30 minutes, plus 10 minutes to steam

4 quarts water

2 teaspoons sea salt

2½ cups long-grain brown rice

1. Bring the water and salt to a boil in a large pot over high heat.

2. When the water is boiling, add the rice and allow to cook uncovered for 30 minutes over medium heat.

3. Turn off the stove. Drain the rice thoroughly in a fine metal strainer. Return the rice to the pot, cover with a tight-fitting lid, and allow to steam for another 10 minutes. Fluff with a fork.

NUTRITION PER SERVING: 86 calories, fat 1g, protein 2g, carbohydrate 18g, fiber 1g

Freezer Friendly: Allow the rice to cool completely and then divide into desired portion sizes and place into zip-top bags. Remove all excess air from the bags and seal. Label and store for up to 3 months in the freezer.

HOW TO RE-HEAT RICE

This book includes several recipes that include rice. For those that don't have specific instructions for cooking the rice, such as fried rice, here is how to reheat it.

1. Place the rice in a heat-proof container and for every cup of rice, add 2 teaspoons of water.

2. Microwave on high for 45 seconds per cup of rice. If you're re-heating more than two cups of rice, stir once or twice throughout the cooking process.

Blanched Green Beans

Cooking green beans in boiling water until bright green and crisp-tender and then shocking them in an ice water bath makes them ready for anything—a tender salad topped with lemon, mint, and almonds, a quick stir-fry with sliced meat, or even a long soak in a simple pickle brine.

YIELD: 8 (1-cup) servings | PREP TIME: 5 minutes | COOK TIME: 4 to 5 minutes

2 pounds green beans, stem ends removed

sea salt

1. Add the sea salt to a large pot of water and bring to a boil over high heat.

2. To prepare an ice water bath, fill a large bowl with cold water and several cups of ice cubes.

3. Cook the green beans in the boiling water for 4 to 5 minutes, until they are bright green. To test for doneness, remove one medium-size green bean from the water and dunk it into the ice water to chill. Bite into it. It should be tender enough not to squeak, but not soft.

4. When the green beans are done, remove the pot from the heat and transfer the vegetables to the ice water bath with tongs or a spider, reserving the boiling water to cook the potatoes in the next recipe.

5. When the green beans have cooled completely, about 5 minutes, drain thoroughly and then transfer to a storage container until ready to serve or use in a recipe.

NUTRITION PER SERVING: 36 calories, fat 0g, protein 2g, carbohydrate 8g, fiber 4g

Boiled Potatoes

Use the green bean cooking water to cook small Yukon Gold potatoes in just 10 minutes. Double the recipe so that you can use them not only in the Vegetarian Niçoise Salad (page 38) but also in breakfast scrambles or sliced over pizza with rosemary, sausage, and olive oil.

YIELD: 4 (1-cup) servings | PREP TIME: 2 minutes | COOK TIME: 12 minutes

1 pound Yukon Gold potatoes, scrubbed, unpeeled

sea salt

1. Add the potatoes to a large pot of salted water and bring to a boil over high heat.

2. Cover and cook for 12 minutes, or until the potatoes are fork tender. Remove them with a spider or a pair of tongs to a separate dish to cool.

NUTRITION PER SERVING: 80 calories, fat 0g, protein 2g, carbohydrate 18g, fiber 3g

Soft-Boiled Eggs

Eggs are a convenient source of protein and can be used to dress up a salad or as a topping for brown rice bowls. That's why I like to sneak a batch of boiled eggs into my weekend prep day.

YIELD: 12 (1-egg) servings | PREP TIME: 5 minutes | COOK TIME: 7 to 10 minutes

1 dozen fresh large eggs

1. Bring a large pot of water to a gentle boil. Add the eggs, cover, and cook for 8 minutes for soft boiled and 11 minutes for hard boiled. (For the recipes this week, cook 4 of them soft boiled and 8 of them hard boiled.)

2. To prepare an ice water bath, fill a large bowl with cold water and several cups of ice cubes. (You can also refresh the water used for shocking the green beans.)

3. Remove the pot from the heat and transfer the eggs to the ice water bath with tongs.

4. When completely cooled, peel the eggs. If the shells are sticking, rinse them under cool running water as you peel.

NUTRITION PER SERVING: 78 calories, fat 5g, protein 6g, carbohydrate <1g, fiber 0g

Salsa Verde

Spicy jalapeno and garlic are whirled into this punchy sauce that's perfect on flank steak or drizzled over salmon. It's also good over beans and rice, chicken, or with soft-boiled eggs. Okay, I'm just so in love with this sauce I'd pour it over anything.

YIELD: 1 cup or 8 (2-tablespoon) servings | PREP TIME: 5 minutes | COOK TIME: 0 minutes

Place all of the ingredients in a blender and puree until mostly smooth. Serve immediately or store in a covered container for up to 3 days in the refrigerator. To prep the sauce for longer storage, place all of the ingredients except the lime juice and oil into a blender container and add the oil and lime juice just before you're ready to serve.

NUTRITION PER SERVING: 63 calories, fat 7g, protein 0g, carbohydrate 1g, fiber <1g

Variation Tip: If you don't like cilantro, replace it with fresh flat-leaf parsley and use 3 tablespoons red wine vinegar instead of the lime juice for a riff on chimichurri.

2 cups packed fresh cilantro

1 large jalapeno pepper, cored and roughly chopped

4 garlic cloves, roughly chopped

2 limes, juiced

¼ cup extra-virgin olive oil

¼ teaspoon sea salt

Hoisin Stir-Fry Sauce

This sauce works for stir-fries or for dipping sticky rice or salad rolls.

YIELD: ½ cup, or 4 (2-tablespoon) servings | PREP TIME: 5 minutes | COOK TIME: 0 minutes

Combine all of the ingredients in a small jar. Cover and shake vigorously to mix.

NUTRITION PER SERVING: 43 calories, fat 1g, protein 1g, carbohydrate 8g, fiber 1g

¼ cup hoisin sauce

2 tablespoons low-sodium, gluten-free soy sauce

2 tablespoons lime juice

1/8 teaspoon crushed red pepper

1 tablespoon minced ginger

1 tablespoon minced garlic

Hoisin Beef and Green Bean Stir-Fry

Stir-fry is already a quick meal, but with all of the ingredients precooked and the sauce mixed, this version comes together in just minutes. Now that's fast food!

YIELD: 4 servings | PREP TIME: 2 minutes | COOK TIME: 2 minutes

1. Heat the oil in a large skillet over high heat. Sauté the green beans for 1 minute.

2. Reduce the heat to medium and add the stir-fry sauce and beef. Simmer until just heated through, about 1 minute. Be careful not to overcook the beef.

3. Garnish with green onions and serve over brown rice.

NUTRITION PER SERVING: 376 calories, fat 15g, protein 29g, carbohydrate 35g, fiber 6g

Freezer Friendly: Prepare the recipe as directed and divide the ingredients between storage containers. Cool, cover, label, and freeze for up to 1 month.

Make Plant Based: To make this recipe plant based, swap the flank steak for one 15-ounce block of tofu. Drain, press, and cut into cubes. Toss with 1 tablespoon of oil and roast in a 425°F oven for 15 minutes.

1 tablespoon canola oil

4 cups halved Blanched Green Beans (page 29)

½ cup Hoisin Stir-Fry Sauce (page 31)

12 ounces Rosemary Garlic Grilled Flank Steak (page 27), thinly sliced on a bias

¼ cup thinly sliced green onions

2 cups Perfectly Cooked Brown Rice (page 28)

Bibimbap

Long before bliss bowls became the darling of clean eating circles, there was bibimbap—a Korean mainstay of steamed rice topped with kimchi, cooked egg, fresh vegetables, and sautéed spinach. It makes the ultimate healthy eating bowl and can be customized to suit each person's taste and dietary preferences. It also comes together really quickly for dinner or can be packed away for a grab-and-go lunch. If kimchi is not your thing, top the bowl with a drizzle of sriracha.

YIELD: **4** servings | PREP TIME: **5** minutes | COOK TIME: **1** minute

4 cups Perfectly Cooked Brown Rice (page 28)

8 ounces Rosemary Garlic Grilled Flank Steak (page 27), minced

4 Soft-Boiled Eggs (page 30)

1 teaspoon toasted sesame oil

8 cups fresh spinach

1 teaspoon minced garlic

1 cup kimchi

¼ cup thinly sliced green onions

1 carrot, grated

low-sodium, gluten-free soy sauce, to serve

1. Heat the steak and brown rice separately in the microwave. Place the eggs in a large bowl of hot water to warm gently.

2. Heat the oil in a large skillet over medium-high heat. Cook the spinach and garlic for about 1 minute or until the spinach is just wilted.

3. Divide the brown rice between serving dishes. Top with sautéed spinach, minced steak, boiled eggs, kimchi, green onions, and grated carrot. Serve with soy sauce.

NUTRITION PER SERVING: 452 calories, fat 15g, protein 30g, carbohydrate 50g, fiber 6g

Make Plant Based: Eight ounces of crumbled tempeh can be used in place of the steak if you prefer. For a completely vegan meal, omit the eggs.

Sautéed Tomato Rice Pilaf with Salsa Verde Salmon

With a good sauce, you can transform everyday ingredients like tomatoes, spinach, and rice into a flavorful pilaf, and salsa verde is the sauce for the job. Top it off with a quick-cooking piece of salmon for an almost instant meal. The dish works just as well with a pan-seared chicken breast, but it takes a little longer to cook.

YIELD: 4 servings | PREP TIME: 5 minutes | COOK TIME: 8 minutes

1. Heat ½ tablespoon of the olive oil in a large skillet over medium-high heat. Pat the salmon fillets dry with paper towels and season generously with salt and pepper.

2. Sear the salmon for about 2 minutes on each side for medium-rare. Place on a warmed plate and cover with foil to keep warm.

3. Add the remaining ½ tablespoon of olive oil to the skillet and cook the garlic and tomatoes for 2 minutes. Add the spinach and brown rice and cook until the spinach is wilted and the brown rice is heated through, about 2 minutes.

4. Divide the rice pilaf between serving bowls and top with a salmon fillet. Drizzle with the salsa verde and top with diced avocado, if you'd like.

NUTRITION PER SERVING: 407 calories, fat 20g, protein 33g, carbohydrate 23g, fiber 5g

1 tablespoon extra-virgin olive oil, divided

16 ounces salmon, cut into four (4-ounce) fillets

1 teaspoon minced garlic

1 pint grape or cherry tomatoes, halved

4 cups roughly chopped spinach

2 cups Perfectly Cooked Brown Rice (page 28)

½ cup Salsa Verde (page 31)

1 avocado, diced, optional

sea salt

freshly ground pepper

Flank Steak Tacos

With all of the ingredients prepped ahead of time, this easy weeknight supper comes together in just minutes. For best results, microwave each of the corn tortillas separately for about 10 seconds to make them soft and pliable.

YIELD: 4 servings | PREP TIME: 5 minutes | COOK TIME: 0 minutes

1. Warm the flank steak and the corn tortillas separately.

2. Divide the steak between each of the tortillas and top with salsa verde, queso fresco, if using, shredded cabbage, and avocado. Serve with lime wedges.

NUTRITION PER SERVING: 512 calories, fat 24g, protein 35g, carbohydrate 39g, fiber 7g

12 ounces Rosemary Garlic Grilled Flank Steak (page 27)

12 corn tortillas

½ cup Salsa Verde (page 31)

4 ounces queso fresco, optional

2 cups shredded cabbage

1 lime, cut into wedges

Vegetarian Niçoise Salad

I love Niçoise salad and am happy to order it in a French restaurant, but at lunchtime, I don't exactly love the idea of searing a piece of tuna. Opening up a jar of anchovies sounds even worse! Instead, when I make it at home, I opt for a vegetarian salad and double up on the boiled eggs, green beans, and potatoes. This makes an excellent lunch or light dinner.

YIELD: 4 servings | PREP TIME: 10 minutes | COOK TIME: 0 minutes

2 tablespoons white wine vinegar

1 teaspoon Dijon mustard

1 shallot, minced

¼ cup extra-virgin olive oil

8 cups mixed baby lettuce

4 cups Blanched Green Beans (page 29), halved

4 cups Boiled Potatoes (page 30), halved

8 Soft-Boiled Eggs

½ cup Niçoise olives

1 pint halved grape or cherry tomatoes

sea salt

freshly ground pepper

1. In a large bowl, whisk the vinegar, mustard, shallot, and olive oil until emulsified. Season with salt and pepper.

2. Add the lettuce, green beans, and potatoes to the bowl and toss gently to coat.

3. Divide the dressed vegetables between serving plates. Top each with two eggs, olives, and a handful of tomatoes.

NUTRITION PER SERVING: 434 calories, fat 26g, protein 19g, carbohydrate 34g, fiber 9g

Serving Tip: A Niçoise salad is often served composed, which is pretty, but I prefer to enjoy it all mixed together so that the dressing flavors each element.

■ ■ ■ ■

PORK AND POLENTA

Now that you've got the hang of preparing foundation recipes once a week, let's infuse some exciting new flavors into the menu. This week features grilled pork tenderloin as the primary protein source. It is paired with a blackberry glaze and a tangy ginger soy vinaigrette. Another sauce that really livens up the menu is romesco, made from roasted red peppers, tomatoes, toasted almonds, and red wine vinegar. I also introduce one of the most leftover-friendly recipes ever: oven-baked polenta fries.

FOUNDATION RECIPES

Grilled Pork Tenderloin

Blackberry Glaze

Creamy Polenta

Blanched Broccolini

Boiled Purple Potatoes

Romesco Sauce

MAIN MEALS

Grilled Pork Tenderloin with Blackberry Glaze over Polenta with Sautéed Broccolini

Polenta Fries with Romesco and Fried Egg

Roasted Red Pepper Soup with Spinach and Cannellini Beans

Pork Tenderloin with Mixed Greens and Purple Potatoes

Vietnamese Rice Noodle Bowl

WEEK 3 SHOPPING LIST

PANTRY STAPLES

- [ ] Canola oil
- [ ] Extra-virgin olive oil
- [ ] Toasted sesame oil
- [ ] Low-sodium soy sauce
- [ ] Red wine vinegar
- [ ] Balsamic vinegar
- [ ] Ground cayenne pepper
- [ ] Crushed red pepper
- [ ] Sugar
- [ ] Sea salt
- [ ] Freshly ground pepper

MEAT, POULTRY, AND FISH

- [ ] 3 pork tenderloins, 4 pounds total

DAIRY AND EGGS

- [ ] 1 stick butter
- [ ] 4 eggs

PACKAGED AND BULK FOODS

- [ ] 2 cups course yellow cornmeal
- [ ] ¼ cup toasted almonds
- [ ] ½ cup toasted cashews
- [ ] 4 ounces thin rice noodles

CANNED GOODS

- [ ] 1 (6-ounce) jar blackberry preserves, preferably seedless
- [ ] 1 (8-ounce) bottle Worcestershire sauce
- [ ] 2 quarts low-sodium chicken broth
- [ ] 1 (15-ounce) can cannellini beans
- [ ] 1 (6-ounce) jar sambal chile paste
- [ ] 1 quart vegetable broth

PRODUCE

- [ ] 1 head garlic
- [ ] 1 small red onion
- [ ] 1 (3-inch) piece ginger
- [ ] 4 bunches broccolini (or 2 heads broccoli)
- [ ] 1 pound purple potatoes
- [ ] 1 bunch fresh rosemary
- [ ] 1 bunch fresh mint
- [ ] 4 large red bell peppers
- [ ] 4 large vine-ripe tomatoes
- [ ] 1 bunch fresh flat-leaf parsley
- [ ] 1 (10-ounce) bag baby spinach
- [ ] 1 (10-ounce bag) mixed salad greens
- [ ] ½ cup dates or raisins
- [ ] 2 limes
- [ ] 1 (8-ounce) package shredded cabbage
- [ ] 1 small cucumber
- [ ] 2 carrots

SAVVY SHORTCUTS

- Buy prepared polenta in a tube.
- Buy roasted red peppers and canned plum tomatoes to prepare the romesco sauce.

Grilled Pork Tenderloin

My church hosts communal dinners for five weeks in the fall and another five weeks in the spring. I love helping in the kitchen, and this is one of our go-to recipes for feeding a crowd. We often have more than 100 guests, so it's important to choose easy, fuss-free recipes that everyone will enjoy. The leftovers are equally delicious, making this pork tenderloin the perfect protein for meal prep.

YIELD: 12 (3-ounce) servings | PREP TIME: 5 minutes, plus 30 minutes inactive time |
COOK TIME: 16 to 18 minutes

2 tablespoons canola oil

2/3 cup low-sodium,
gluten-free soy sauce

1/3 tablespoon red wine vinegar

1 tablespoon minced garlic

1 tablespoon minced ginger

½ teaspoon ground cayenne

3 pork tenderloins,
approximately 4 pounds total

1. Light a charcoal or gas grill, or preheat a grill pan. If you're using gas or a pan, you can wait to do this step until just before you're ready to cook.

2. Whisk the canola oil, soy sauce, vinegar, garlic, ginger, and cayenne in a large, non-reactive baking dish. Add the pork tenderloin and turn to coat the meat in the marinade. Set aside to marinate for 30 minutes, or place in the refrigerator and marinate overnight.

3. When the grill is hot, remove the tenderloins from the marinade and place them on the grill. Cook for about 4 minutes on all sides (for a total of 16 to 18 minutes), or until cooked through to an internal temperature of 145°F.

4. Allow the pork to rest for 10 minutes before slicing into 1-inch thick medallions.

NUTRITION PER SERVING: 171 calories, fat 7g, protein 25g, carbohydrate 0g, fiber 0g

Freezer Friendly: Allow the sliced pork to cool completely. Divide it into individual portions and place into zip-top plastic bags. Remove as much air as possible from the bags before sealing. Label and freeze until ready to use.

Blackberry Glaze

This sauce gets rave reviews and it's surprisingly easy to make! It can be served over pork tenderloin, as suggested, or drizzled over salads.

YIELD: 1 cup | PREP TIME: 5 minutes | COOK TIME: 5 minutes

Place all of the ingredients into a sauce pan and bring to a gentle simmer for 5 minutes, until slightly thickened. Cool and cover in an airtight container until ready to serve.

NUTRITION PER (2-TABLESPOON) SERVING: 71 calories, fat 0g, protein 0g, carbohydrate 18g, fiber 0g

Make Gluten Free: To make this gluten-free and vegan, choose a gluten-free Worcestershire sauce without anchovies.

2/3 cup seedless blackberry preserves

¼ cup balsamic vinegar

2 tablespoons Worcestershire sauce

sea salt

freshly ground pepper

Creamy Polenta

Homemade polenta has a reputation for being labor intensive, but it really doesn't have to be. Think about it this way—you can prepare rice or risotto. One version requires about 2 minutes of hands-on cooking; the other takes about 30 minutes of constant supervision. Good polenta is somewhere in between. You should stir it for the first 10 minutes or so, but then you can cover the pot and let it continue cooking for another 15 to 20 minutes, only stirring occasionally.

YIELD: 8 (1-cup) servings | PREP TIME: 5 minutes | COOK TIME: 25 to 30 minutes

8 cups water or low-sodium chicken broth (see page 14 for homemade stock)

1 teaspoon sea salt

2 cups coarse yellow cornmeal (sometimes labeled polenta)

3 tablespoons butter, divided

1. In a large pot over medium-low heat, bring the water or broth and salt to a simmer.

2. Pour in the cornmeal in a thin, steady stream, whisking constantly.

3. Reduce the heat to low and continue stirring for about 10 minutes. Cover the pot and cook for another 15 to 20 minutes, stirring a few times throughout to make sure it cooks evenly.

4. Stir in 2 tablespoons of the butter. It can be enjoyed immediately, or to store, use the remaining tablespoon of butter to coat an 8 x 8-inch casserole dish. Pour about half of the polenta into the baking dish and cover loosely with parchment paper or plastic wrap.

NUTRITION PER SERVING: 168 calories, fat 5g, protein 3g, carbohydrate 27g, fiber 2g

Blanched Broccolini

I find I'm far more likely to eat vegetables if they're prepared ahead of time, and blanching and shocking is one of the best ways to do this. Blanched broccolini is especially versatile—you can coat it in a bit of olive oil and grill it until gently charred, sauté it with garlic and crushed red pepper, or serve it with a simple Romesco Sauce (page 47). Of course, broccoli is an acceptable substitute. Simply slice each broccoli crown into quarters lengthwise and prepare as directed.

YIELD: 8 (½-bunch) servings | PREP TIME: 5 minutes | COOK TIME: 2 minutes

1. Bring a large pot of salted water to a boil over high heat.

2. To prepare an ice water bath, fill a large bowl with cold water and several cups of ice cubes.

3. Cook the broccolini in the boiling water for 2 minutes, until it is bright green. To test for doneness, remove one small spear of the broccolini from the water and dunk it into the ice water to chill. Bite into it. It should be tender enough not to squeak, but not soft.

4. When the broccolini is done, remove the pot from the heat and transfer the vegetables to the ice water bath with tongs or a spider. Reserve the cooking liquid.

5. When the broccolini has cooled completely, about 5 minutes, drain thoroughly and then transfer to a storage container until ready to serve or use in a recipe.

NUTRITION PER SERVING: 35 calories, fat 0g, protein 4g, carbohydrate 7g, fiber 4g

Cooking Tip: You can blanch other vegetables in a similar manner. Adjust the cooking time based on the density and thickness of the vegetable. Start with the mildest flavored vegetables first, moving on to the fuller-flavored vegetables (Brussels sprouts, asparagus, broccoli, etc.) as you go. Don't discard that cooking liquid! It can be used as a base for soups or to cook starches, such as rice, pasta, or potatoes.

4 bunches broccolini, ends snapped off

sea salt

Boiled Purple Potatoes

Purple potatoes are a good source of antioxidants and provide a nice color contrast on your plate. They're also delicious roasted. If you prefer that option, follow the instructions for Herb Roasted Potatoes (page 13) but reduce the cooking time to just 15 minutes. The purple variety cooks quickly.

YIELD: **4 servings** | PREP TIME: **2 minutes** | COOK TIME: **12 minutes**

1 pound purple potatoes

1 sprig fresh rosemary

1. Place the potatoes and rosemary into the cooking pot from the broccolini and bring to a boil. Cover and cook for 12 minutes, or until the potatoes are just tender.

2. Drain in a colander. Store in a covered container in the refrigerator.

NUTRITION PER SERVING: 110 calories, fat 0g, protein 3g, carbohydrate 26g, fiber 2g

Romesco Sauce

The first time I made this sauce, I thought, "Wow, this is so good I could drink it!" So, not only does it appear in the Polenta Fries with Romesco and Fried Egg (page 51), but it's also the star of the show in the Roasted Red Pepper Soup with Spinach and Cannellini Beans (page 54). It makes a tasty condiment for scrambled eggs, or is lovely slathered over crusty bread.

YIELD: 12 (¼-cup) servings | PREP TIME: 5 minutes | COOK TIME: 15 minutes

1. Preheat the oven to 425°F.

2. Place the bell peppers, tomatoes, and unpeeled garlic cloves on a rimmed baking sheet and toss with 1 tablespoon of the olive oil. Roast for 15 minutes, tossing once or twice to brown on all sides.

3. Peel the garlic cloves. Place the roasted peppers, tomatoes, and garlic into a blender along with the additional 3 teaspoons olive oil, almonds, red wine vinegar, parsley, and sugar, if using. (It is helpful during the off-season months when tomatoes are not as flavorful.)

4. Blend until somewhat smooth but still textured.

5. Store in a covered container in the refrigerator until ready to serve.

NUTRITION PER SERVING: 88 calories, fat 6g, protein 2g, carbohydrate 8g, fiber 2g

4 large red bell peppers, cored, seeded, and quartered

4 large vine-ripe tomatoes, quartered and seeded

4 garlic cloves, unpeeled

4 tablespoons extra-virgin olive oil, divided

¼ cup roughly chopped toasted almonds

½ cup red wine vinegar

¼ cup fresh flat-leaf parsley

pinch sugar, optional

Grilled Pork Tenderloin with Blackberry Glaze over Polenta

If you mistook this meal for something you would order in a restaurant and happily pay good money for, I wouldn't blame you! It's fine dining and comfort food all at the same time. Bonus, even kids will devour it thanks to the sweet blackberry glaze. Serve with the Sautéed Broccolini with Garlic and Crushed Red Pepper (page 49). I prefer to serve this meal on the same day I do my meal prepping so that I do not have to reheat it. Leftovers can be stored in a meal-prep container and reheated in the microwave until heated through, about two minutes.

YIELD: 4 servings | PREP TIME: 5 minutes | COOK TIME: 0 minutes

12 ounces Grilled Pork Tenderloin (page 42)

4 cups Creamy Polenta (page 44)

½ cup Blackberry Glaze (page 43)

Divide the polenta between serving dishes. Top each portion with the pork medallions and 2 tablespoons of the blackberry glaze.

NUTRITION PER SERVING: 410 calories, fat 12g, protein 28g, carbohydrate 45g, fiber 2g

Freezer Friendly: Place the covered meal-prep container in the freezer. Remove 24 hours before you wish to serve the meal. Microwave until hot.

Sautéed Broccolini with Garlic and Crushed Red Pepper

Serve this sautéed broccolini alongside the Grilled Pork Tenderloin with Blackberry Glaze over Polenta (page 48) and with Polenta Fries with Romesco and Fried Egg (page 51). The recipe below yields four servings and can be made twice this week to serve with both meals.

YIELD: 4 servings | PREP TIME: 2 minutes | COOK TIME: 3 minutes

1. Heat a large skillet over medium-high heat. Add the olive oil.

2. When it is hot, add the broccolini. Cook until the broccolini is nearly heated through, about 2 minutes. Add the garlic and crushed red pepper and cook for 30 seconds, or just until fragrant. Sprinkle with the red wine vinegar and season with salt.

1 tablespoon extra-virgin olive oil

2 bunches Blanched Broccolini (page 45)

1 teaspoon minced garlic

pinch crushed red pepper

½ tablespoon red wine vinegar

sea salt

NUTRITION PER SERVING: 65 calories, fat 4g, protein 4g, carbohydrate 7g, fiber 4g

Polenta Fries with Romesco and Fried Egg

Transform cold polenta into a trendy restaurant staple in this simple, vegetarian dinner. To make this a fully grab-and-go meal, you may want to make Soft-Boiled Eggs (page 30) and skip the sautéed broccolini—simply add the blanched broccolini to the meal.

YIELD: 4 servings | PREP TIME: 5 minutes | COOK TIME: 20 minutes

1. Preheat the oven to 400°F. Line a rimmed baking sheet with parchment paper.

2. Spread the polenta out on the baking sheet and drizzle with 1 tablespoon of the olive oil, tossing very gently to coat the polenta spears in the oil. Season with salt. Roast for 20 minutes, until gently browned.

3. While the polenta cooks, sauté the broccolini according to the recipe instructions.

4. About 5 minutes before the polenta is done, heat a large skillet over medium-high heat.

5. Add the remaining olive oil. When it is hot, crack each of the eggs into the pan and fry for 4 minutes, or until the whites are set but the yolks are still runny. Season with salt.

6. To serve, divide the warmed romesco between serving plates. Top with polenta fries, broccolini, and fried egg.

NUTRITION PER SERVING: 393 calories, fat 20g, protein 15g, carbohydrate 42g, fiber 8g

4 cups chilled Creamy Polenta (page 44), sliced into 1 x 4-inch-thick spears

2 tablespoons extra-virgin olive oil, divided

1 recipe Sautéed Broccolini with Garlic and Crushed Red Pepper (page 49)

4 eggs

1 cup Romesco Sauce (page 47), warmed

sea salt

Pork Tenderloin with Mixed Greens and Purple Potatoes

This salad has two dressings. The first is a simple red wine and rosemary vinaigrette to coat the salad greens and onion. The second is a sweet Blackberry Glaze drizzled over the top of the salad. The pungent rosemary in the first dressing really plays well with the blackberry. If you prefer a hot meal, you can warm the potatoes and pork before serving.

YIELD: 4 servings | PREP TIME: 5 minutes | COOK TIME: 0 minutes

1 tablespoon red wine vinegar

2 tablespoons extra-virgin olive oil

1 teaspoon minced fresh rosemary

¼ teaspoon sea salt

12 cups mixed salad greens

1 small red onion, halved and thinly sliced

½ cup pitted and chopped dates or raisins

12 ounces Grilled Pork Tenderloin (page 42)

4 cups Boiled Purple Potatoes (page 46), halved

½ cup Blackberry Glaze (page 43)

1. Whisk the vinegar, olive oil, rosemary, and sea salt in a large mixing bowl. Add the salad greens and red onion, and toss gently to coat. Divide the greens between salad plates.

2. Top each plate with dates, pork slices, and purple potatoes. Drizzle with the blackberry glaze.

NUTRITION PER SERVING: 563 calories, fat 10g, protein 34g, carbohydrate 85g, fiber 8g

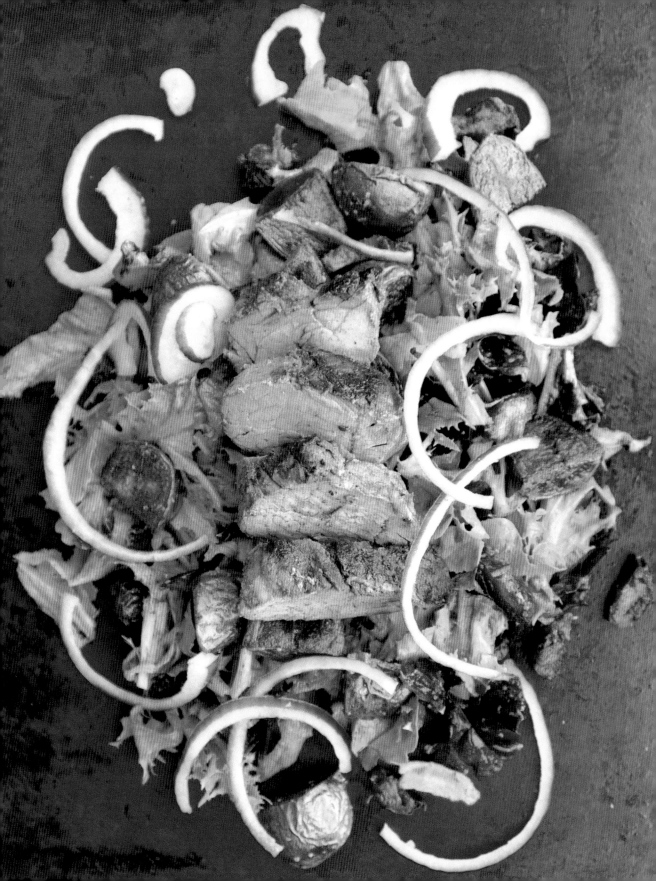

Roasted Red Pepper Soup with Spinach and Cannellini Beans

The Romesco Sauce makes a flavorful base for this simple soup. It comes together in just minutes on the stovetop and can easily be added to your prep-day schedule if you want to get it done ahead of time. Serve with whole grain bread and olive oil.

YIELD: **4 servings** | PREP TIME: **2 minutes** | COOK TIME: **5 minutes**

2 cups Romesco Sauce (page 47)

1 quart vegetable broth

1 (8-ounce) bag baby spinach

2 (15-ounce) cans cannellini beans, rinsed and drained

sea salt

freshly ground pepper

1. Place the Romesco Sauce and vegetable broth into a large pot and bring to a simmer.

2. Add the spinach and cannellini beans and cook until the spinach is wilted and the beans are heated through, about 2 minutes.

NUTRITION PER SERVING: 387 calories, fat 6g, protein 20g, carbohydrate 60g, fiber g

Vietnamese Rice Noodle Bowl

Rice noodles are a convenient starch to add to any meal because unlike pasta made with wheat, rice noodles are already cooked and simply need to be soaked in hot water for 10 minutes then drained. You can add this to your prep day schedule or simply soak the noodles while you chop the other ingredients.

YIELD: 4 servings | PREP TIME: 10 minutes | COOK TIME: 0 minutes

1. Fill a large heat-proof bowl with hot water. Place the rice noodles into the water and soak for 10 minutes. Drain thoroughly.

2. While the noodles are soaking, whisk the soy sauce, sesame oil, lime juice, chile paste, and ginger together in a small jar.

3. Divide the noodles between serving bowls and drizzle with the soy lime vinaigrette. Toss gently to mix.

4. Top the noodles with pork slices, cabbage, carrot, cucumber, mint, and cashews.

NUTRITION PER SERVING: 376 calories, fat 19g, protein 31g, carbohydrate 22g, fiber 3g

4 ounces thin rice noodles (not the wide flat noodles)

¼ cup low-sodium, gluten-free soy sauce

1 tablespoon toasted sesame oil

2 tablespoons lime juice

1 teaspoon sambal chile paste

1 teaspoon minced ginger

12 ounces Grilled Pork Tenderloin (page 42), sliced

2 cups shredded cabbage

1 cup grated carrot

1 small cucumber, sliced

handful fresh mint leaves

½ cup chopped toasted cashews

WEEK 4

■ ■ ■ ■

BOWLED OVER

The inspiration for this week's menu is one of my favorite restaurants when I'm on the go. I love eating there on family road trips or after a good surf session when I have little interest in cooking my own food from scratch. But, if I had all of the ingredients prepped ahead of time, I could create my own spicy flavored bowls (or burritos) in as much time as it takes to go through the line and whip out my credit card. This week, I take some of the restaurant's staples and transform them into easy make-ahead meals.

FOUNDATION RECIPES

Cilantro Lime Rice

Roasted Sweet Potatoes

Roasted Peppers and Onions

Spicy Pinto Beans

Corn Salsa

Pico de Gallo

MAIN MEALS

Loaded Bean and Rice Bowls

Tortilla Soup

Mexican Shakshuka

New York Strip Steak with
Sweet Potato Salad

Chile Lime Halibut with
Corn Salsa and Rice

WEEK 4 SHOPPING LIST

PANTRY STAPLES

- [ ] Canola oil
- [ ] Sherry vinegar
- [ ] Maple syrup, honey, or agave
- [ ] Ground cumin
- [ ] Dried oregano
- [ ] Smoked paprika
- [ ] Cayenne pepper, optional
- [ ] Garlic powder
- [ ] Sea salt
- [ ] Freshly ground pepper

MEAT, POULTRY, AND FISH

- [ ] 1 pound fresh halibut
- [ ] 16 ounces New York strip steak

DAIRY AND EGGS

- [ ] 4 eggs
- [ ] 2 cups shredded cheddar cheese

FROZEN

- [ ] 1 (16-ounce) package frozen corn kernels

DELI

- [ ] 1 (8-ounce) container prepared guacamole

PACKAGED AND BULK FOODS

- [ ] 1 (16-ounce) package long-grain white rice (2 cups)
- [ ] 1 package corn tortillas (minimum 10 count)
- [ ] 1 bag tortilla chips

CANNED GOODS

- [ ] 3 (29-ounce) cans pinto beans, drained but not rinsed
- [ ] 32 ounces (4 cups) vegetable broth or chicken broth
- [ ] 1 (15-ounce) can fire-roasted diced tomatoes

PRODUCE

- [ ] 4 red bell peppers
- [ ] 4 green bell peppers
- [ ] 2 yellow onions
- [ ] 2 red onions
- [ ] 1 head garlic
- [ ] 2 jalapeno peppers
- [ ] 2 bunches fresh cilantro
- [ ] 1 bunch fresh flat-leaf parsley
- [ ] 5 limes
- [ ] 2 pounds sweet potatoes
- [ ] 1 pound tomatoes
- [ ] 1 head romaine or red leaf lettuce
- [ ] 1 shallot
- [ ] 2 avocados

SAVVY SHORTCUTS

- Buy prepared pico de gallo.
- Buy frozen precooked or instant white rice.

Cilantro Lime Rice

Liven up basic white rice with a hint of lime and cilantro. It can also be made with brown rice—increase the water to 4 cups and increase the cooking time to 30 minutes.

YIELD: 12 (½-cup) servings | PREP TIME: 5 minutes | COOK TIME: 20 minutes

2 cups long-grain white rice

2¾ cups water

1 teaspoon sea salt

1 lime, zest and juice

¼ cup minced cilantro, optional

1. Place the rice into a large pot. Add the sea salt and water. Bring to a simmer. Cover and cook over low heat for 15 minutes. Fluff with a fork.

2. Add the lime zest and juice and minced cilantro, if using. Mix to incorporate.

NUTRITION PER SERVING: 112 calories, fat 0g, protein 2g, carbohydrate 25g, fiber 0g

Freezer Friendly: Divide rice into desired portion sizes and freeze in individual zip-top bags. Mark the date and quantity on the outside of the bags.

Roasted Sweet Potatoes

Like all of the foundation recipes in this book, this one can be taken in so many different directions. Roasted sweet potatoes are delicious in soups, as a filling for burritos, or in a chilled sweet potato salad.

YIELD: 4 (½-cup) servings | PREP TIME: 5 minutes | COOK TIME: 30 minutes

2 pounds sweet potatoes, scrubbed and cut into ½-inch pieces

1 tablespoon canola oil

½ teaspoon sea salt

Preheat the oven to 400°F. Spread the sweet potatoes onto a rimmed baking sheet. Drizzle with the canola oil. Roast for 30 minutes, or until the sweet potatoes are gently browned on the bottoms and shrunken.

NUTRITION PER SERVING: 112 calories, fat 2g, protein 2g, carbohydrate 23g, fiber 3g

Roasted Peppers and Onions

These roasted peppers and onions are so versatile—they can fill everything from burritos to omelets. Roasting them ahead of time amps up their flavor, so you can build a variety of appetizing meals in just minutes.

YIELD: 16 (½-cup) servings | PREP TIME: 10 minutes | COOK TIME: 25 to 30 minutes

4 red bell peppers

4 green bell peppers

2 yellow onions, halved and sliced in ½-inch-thick slices

2 tablespoons canola oil

½ teaspoon sea salt

Preheat the oven to 400°F. Spread the peppers and onions onto a rimmed baking sheet. Drizzle with the canola oil. Roast for 25 to 30 minutes, or until the peppers are deeply browned but not charred.

NUTRITION PER SERVING: 44 calories, fat 2g, protein 1g, carbohydrate 7g, fiber 2g

Roasted Red Peppers and Onions

Spicy Pinto Beans

These savory, spicy pinto beans are adapted from a recipe by Eddie Garza, a Mexican-American chef who crafts the most amazing plant-based recipes. This version yields a significant amount more and uses more accessible ingredients, making it a good meal prep standby.

YIELD: 9 (1-cup) servings | PREP TIME: 10 minutes | COOK TIME: 40 minutes

1 tablespoon canola oil

1 cup minced red onion

2 teaspoons minced garlic

1 tablespoon minced jalapeno pepper

1 tablespoon ground cumin

1 teaspoon dried oregano

1 tablespoon smoked paprika

1/8 teaspoon cayenne pepper, optional

3 (29-ounce) cans pinto beans, drained but not rinsed

½ teaspoon sea salt

2 tablespoons lime juice

¼ cup minced roughly chopped fresh cilantro

1. Heat the canola oil in a large, deep skillet over medium-high heat. Cook the onion until it picks up some color and begins to soften, about 5 minutes. Reduce the heat to medium.

2. Add the garlic, jalapeno, cumin, oregano, paprika, and cayenne, if using. Cook for 30 seconds, just until fragrant.

3. Add the beans and salt, and cook for 2 to 3 minutes, until heated through. Stir in the lime juice and cilantro.

NUTRITION PER SERVING: 98 calories, fat 2g, protein 9g, carbohydrate 11g, fiber 2g

Ingredient Tip: To use dry beans, soak <u>one pound</u> of dry pinto beans in fresh water overnight. Rinse and drain. Place in a large pot and cover with about 2 inches of water. Simmer for 1 hour, or until the beans are soft.

Corn Salsa

This crunchy corn salsa is amazing when you make it from fresh ears of corn, but the point of meal prepping is to make life easier, not harder. So, unless corn is in season and you have time to spare, frozen corn will work just fine. For extra flavor, opt for roasted corn kernels.

YIELD: 12 (¼-cup) servings | PREP TIME: 5 minutes | COOK TIME: 0 minutes

1 cup diced red onion

2 cups frozen corn kernels, defrosted under cool running water

2 tablespoons minced jalapeno pepper

1 tablespoon lime juice

¼ cup minced fresh cilantro

sea salt

freshly ground pepper

Combine all of the ingredients and season with salt and pepper to taste.

NUTRITION PER SERVING: 28 calories, fat 0g, protein 1g, carbohydrate 6g, fiber 1g

Pico de Gallo

You can certainly purchase pico de gallo from the deli section of your supermarket, but it's so easy to make and the flavors are exceptional when prepared from scratch. Bonus, it's a fraction of the price.

YIELD: 12 (¼-cup) servings | PREP TIME: 5 minutes | COOK TIME: 0 minutes

Combine all of the ingredients and season with salt and pepper to taste.

NUTRITION PER SERVING: 10 calories, fat 0g, protein 0g, carbohydrate 2g, fiber 1g

2 cups diced tomatoes

½ cup diced red onion

½ cup minced fresh cilantro

1 tablespoon minced jalapeno

2 tablespoons lime juice

sea salt

freshly ground pepper

Loaded Bean and Rice Bowls

I love eating at Chipotle when I'm traveling. I can usually count on getting something healthy and delicious and each person in my family gets to customize their own bowl. These bean and rice bowls are inspired by what I typically order at the restaurant. Feel free to add shredded cheese and sour cream if you need more calories in the dish.

YIELD: **4 servings** | PREP TIME: **5 minutes** | COOK TIME: **0 minutes**

2 cups Cilantro Lime Rice (page 58)

2 cups Roasted Peppers and Onions (page 60)

4 cups Spicy Pinto Beans (page 62)

1 cup Corn Salsa (page 64)

1 cup Pico de Gallo (page 65)

4 cups shredded lettuce

1 cup prepared guacamole, optional

Divide the ingredients between serving bowls and serve immediately.

NUTRITION PER SERVING: 357 calories, fat 9g, protein 14g, carbohydrate 54g, fiber 8g

Tortilla Soup

Roasting the peppers and onions ahead of time brings a depth of flavor to this soup that would otherwise be unattainable in just 10 minutes. You can also add this main meal recipe to your prep-day schedule so that it is completely ready to go when you want to serve it.

YIELD: 4 servings | PREP TIME: 5 minutes | COOK TIME: 10 minutes

2 cups Roasted Peppers and Onions (page 60)

32 ounces (4 cups) vegetable broth or chicken broth (see page 14 for homemade)

2 corn tortillas, hand torn

1 (15-ounce) can fire-roasted diced tomatoes

2 cups shredded cheddar cheese

1 avocado, thinly sliced

1 cup Pico de Gallo (page 65)

tortilla chips, to serve

1. Place the roasted peppers and onions, broth, corn tortillas, and fire-roasted diced tomatoes in a medium pot and bring to a simmer for 10 minutes. Use an immersion blender or carefully transfer the mixture to a standard blender and puree until smooth.

2. Divide the soup between serving bowls and top with cheddar cheese, avocado, and pico de gallo. Serve with tortilla chips.

NUTRITION PER SERVING: 372 calories, fat 25g, protein 18g, carbohydrate 20g, fiber 6g

Make Plant Based: Use vegetable broth and a vegan shredded cheddar cheese, such as Follow Your Heart brand, to make this recipe plant based.

Mexican Shakshuka

This recipe blends North African shakshuka with Mexican huevos rancheros for a flavorful way to transform leftovers into a delicious meal. Shakshuka is a dish of eggs poached in simmering peppers, tomatoes, and onions. Huevos rancheros brings beans, salsa, and avocado to the party.

YIELD: 4 servings | PREP TIME: 5 minutes | COOK TIME: 10 minutes

1. Preheat the oven to 375°F.

2. Heat the peppers and onions and spicy pinto beans in a large cast iron skillet over medium heat until nearly simmering, about 2 minutes total.

3. Make four small indentations in the mixture and crack an egg into each one. Season with salt and pepper. Transfer the pan to the oven and cook for 7 to 8 minutes, or until the eggs are set.

4. Sprinkle the diced avocado and cilantro over the top. Serve with pico de gallo and warmed corn tortillas.

NUTRITION PER SERVING: 412 calories, fat 16g, protein 21g, carbohydrate 52g, fiber 12g

4 cups Roasted Peppers and Onions (page 60)

4 cups Spicy Pinto Beans (page 62)

4 eggs

1 avocado, diced

handful fresh cilantro, roughly chopped

½ cup Pico de Gallo (page 65)

8 corn tortillas, warmed, to serve

sea salt

freshly ground pepper

Chile Lime Halibut with Corn Salsa and Rice

Smoked paprika, garlic, and cumin coat firm halibut steaks in this balanced dinner. Use garlic powder instead of fresh garlic to keep it from burning during the quick pan sear. Swap the halibut for whatever firm white fish is available at your local market. Scallops are also delicious here and cook in just 5 minutes. I like to serve the rice chilled, but you can reheat it in the microwave with 1 tablespoon of water for 1 to 2 minutes if you prefer it warm.

YIELD: 4 servings | PREP TIME: 5 minutes | COOK TIME: 5 minutes

1 teaspoon smoked paprika

½ teaspoon garlic powder

¼ teaspoon ground cumin

1 lime, zested then
cut into wedges

½ teaspoon sea salt

½ teaspoon freshly
ground pepper

1 pound fresh halibut, cut
into 4 fillets or steaks

1 tablespoon canola oil

2 cups Cilantro Lime
Rice (page 58)

2 cups Corn Salsa (page 64)

1. Mix the smoked paprika, garlic powder, cumin, lime zest, salt, and pepper in a small bowl.

2. Pat the halibut fillets dry with paper towels and then season with the spice blend.

3. Heat a large skillet over medium-high heat. Add the canola oil to the pan. When it is hot, sear the halibut for 2 to 3 minutes on each side, or until the fish flakes easily with a fork and is opaque throughout.

4. Divide the rice and corn salsa between serving dishes and top with the cooked halibut.

5. Garnish with the lime wedges.

NUTRITION PER SERVING: 358 calories, fat 7g, protein 32g, carbohydrate 37g, fiber 2g

New York Strip Steak with Sweet Potato Salad

New York strip steaks are flavorful, tender, and cook in a flash. Pair with a complex sweet potato salad for a complete meal.

YIELD: 4 servings | PREP TIME: 10 minutes | COOK TIME: 5 minutes

½ cup minced fresh flat-leaf parsley

2 tablespoons minced shallots

2 tablespoons sherry vinegar or red wine vinegar

1 teaspoon maple syrup, honey, or agave

4 cups Roasted Sweet Potatoes (page 60)

1 tablespoon canola oil

16 ounces New York strip steak

sea salt

freshly ground pepper

1. Mix the parsley, shallots, vinegar, and maple syrup in a large serving bowl. Season with salt and pepper. Add the roasted sweet potatoes and toss to mix. Set aside.

2. Heat a large skillet over medium-high heat. When it is hot, add the canola oil.

3. Pat the steak dry with paper towels and season liberally with salt and pepper.

4. Sear the steak for about 4 to 5 minutes on each side for medium-rare. Transfer the cooked steak to a cutting board and allow to rest for 5 minutes before slicing into ½-inch slices. Serve alongside the sweet potato salad.

NUTRITION PER SERVING: 487 calories, fat 22g, protein 29g, carbohydrate 48g, fiber 6g

WEEK 5

■ ■ ■ ■

GRAB-AND-GO MIXED GRILL

This week is all about simple, grab-and-go meals. During the prep day, you will prepare all of the foundation recipes as usual, but if you feel like assembling all of the meals completely, they're designed to heat and serve, or even to enjoy chilled.

The grill or a grill pan does the heavy lifting cooking the chicken and shrimp, while tofu gets roasted in the oven for a chewy, crisp exterior. If you're skittish about tofu and have never tried it this way, give it a try. But, if you want to skip it, add an extra pound of chicken to the grill and use that in place of tofu.

FOUNDATION RECIPES

Roasted Fajita Vegetables

Crispy Roasted Tofu

Steamed Black Rice

Grilled Chicken Breast

Grilled Lemon Paprika Shrimp

MAIN MEALS

Black Rice Pilaf with Grilled
Shrimp and Peppers

Kale Salad with Grilled Chicken
and Citrus Vinaigrette

Chicken Fajita Bowl with
Avocado Lime Dressing

Mango, Tofu, and Snap Pea "Stir-Fry"

Spicy Salad Roll in a Bowl

WEEK 5 SHOPPING LIST

PANTRY STAPLES

- [ ] Canola oil
- [ ] Extra-virgin olive oil
- [ ] Toasted sesame oil
- [ ] Low-sodium soy sauce
- [ ] Red wine vinegar
- [ ] Sugar, maple syrup, or honey
- [ ] Cornstarch
- [ ] Smoked paprika
- [ ] Crushed red pepper
- [ ] Sea salt
- [ ] Freshly ground black pepper

MEAT, POULTRY, AND FISH

- [ ] 3 pounds boneless, skinless chicken breast
- [ ] 1 pound peeled, deveined jumbo shrimp

DELI

- [ ] 2 (14-ounce) packages extra-firm tofu

PACKAGED AND BULK FOODS

- [ ] 4 ounces (½ cup) toasted cashews
- [ ] 4 cups black rice

CANNED GOODS

- [ ] 1 jar sambal chile paste

PRODUCE

- [ ] 4 medium sweet potatoes, about 28 ounces
- [ ] 2 large mangoes, 1 (16-ounce) bag frozen mangoes, or 1 (16-ounce) jar mangoes
- [ ] 4 red bell peppers
- [ ] 4 green bell peppers
- [ ] 1 bunch green onions
- [ ] 1 bunch radishes
- [ ] 4 lemons
- [ ] 8 limes
- [ ] 4 kumquats or 1 small orange
- [ ] 2 bunches kale (or 12 cups bagged kale salad)
- [ ] 1 head butter or romaine lettuce
- [ ] 1 (8-ounce) bag shredded cabbage (preferably red)
- [ ] 4 small avocados
- [ ] 1 red onion
- [ ] 14 ounces (4 cups) sugar snap peas

SAVVY SHORTCUTS

- Buy precooked grilled chicken breast.
- Buy precooked shrimp.
- Buy frozen roasted vegetables.

Roasted Fajita Vegetables

Roasted sweet potatoes, peppers, and onions are spiced with smoked paprika. They are excellent as a filling for fajitas or enchiladas, a topping for salad, or in the Chicken Fajita Bowl with Avocado Lime Dressing.

YIELD: **4 servings** | PREP TIME: **10 minutes** | COOK TIME: **20 to 25 minutes**

1. Preheat the oven to 375°F. Line a rimmed baking sheet with parchment paper.

2. Toss the sweet potatoes, red bell peppers, green bell peppers, and red onion with the canola oil and season with the smoked paprika. Spread the vegetables onto the baking sheet. Season generously with salt.

3. Roast for 20 to 25 minutes, or until the sweet potatoes are soft and the peppers are beginning to brown.

NUTRITION PER SERVING: 254 calories, fat 8g, protein 4g, carbohydrate 45g, fiber 7g

4 medium sweet potatoes, diced

2 red bell peppers, thinly sliced

2 green bell peppers, thinly sliced

1 red onion, thinly sliced

2 tablespoons canola oil

2 teaspoons smoked paprika

sea salt

Crispy Roasted Tofu

This might just be the dish that makes you rethink tofu. It certainly was in my house. I had tried pan-frying it but found it to be a hassle. When I discovered this method, I never went back. The tofu dries out slightly in the oven (in a good way) and becomes crisp on the outside and pleasantly chewy. Feel free to use toasted sesame oil and add a splash of soy sauce or sriracha to your tofu before coating it in the cornstarch and oil.

YIELD: 4 (6-ounce) servings | PREP TIME: 5 minutes | COOK TIME: 15 minutes

2 (14-ounce) blocks extra-firm tofu, drained, pressed, and cut into 1-inch cubes

1½ tablespoons cornstarch

½ teaspoon sea salt

1½ tablespoons canola oil

1. Preheat the oven to 400°F. Line a rimmed baking sheet with parchment paper.

2. Place the tofu into a large mixing bowl. Add the cornstarch and sea salt and toss very gently to coat the tofu. You don't want to break it.

3. Add the canola oil and toss gently to coat. Spread the tofu out onto the lined baking sheet and bake for 15 minutes.

NUTRITION PER SERVING: 197 calories, fat 14g, protein 16g, carbohydrate 6g, fiber 2g

Ingredient Tip: To press tofu, slice each block in half horizontally. Lay them in a single layer on a cutting board. Place a second cutting board on top and then set several heavy books or a cast iron skillet on top of the second cutting board. Allow the tofu to rest for at least 10 minutes. For less mess, line the cutting boards with several layers of paper towels. Personally, I prefer to save the paper and just wipe down my countertops afterward.

Steamed Black Rice

For a nice change of color and texture, not to mention a big antioxidant boost, try black rice, also known as forbidden rice because it was traditionally reserved for royalty.

YIELD: 12 (½-cup) servings | PREP TIME: 2 minutes | COOK TIME: 30 to 35 minutes

1. Place the rice, water, and salt in a large pot and bring to a simmer over high heat.

2. Reduce the heat to low, cover the pot with a lid, and cook for 30 to 35 minutes, or until the rice is tender. It will still be pleasantly chewy when fully cooked.

NUTRITION PER SERVING: 160 calories, fat 2g, protein 5g, carbohydrate 34g, fiber 2g

3 cups black rice
5½ cups water
1 teaspoon sea salt

Grilled Chicken Breast

After grilling burgers on the weekend, I like to toss a few seasoned chicken breasts on the grill to get a head start on meal prepping for the week. The few minutes of extra effort save me the time of heating up a grill pan or lighting the grill for just one purpose. If you have the time, soak the chicken in the marinade for up to 8 hours in the refrigerator.

YIELD: 12 (3-ounce) servings | PREP TIME: 5 minutes, plus 30 minutes inactive time | COOK TIME: 15 minutes

¼ cup red wine vinegar

2 tablespoons canola oil

1 teaspoon sea salt

1 teaspoon freshly ground pepper

3 pounds boneless, skinless chicken breast

1. Light a charcoal or gas grill, or preheat a grill pan. If you're using gas or a pan, you can wait to do this step until just before you're ready to cook.

2. Whisk the red wine vinegar, canola oil, salt, and pepper in a large non-reactive dish.

3. Place the chicken breasts into the marinade and turn to coat. Allow to soak for at least 30 minutes, while the grill heats.

4. When the grill is hot, shake the excess marinade from the chicken breasts and place them on the grill. Cook for 7 to 8 minutes on each side, or until cooked through to an internal temperature of 165°F.

NUTRITION PER SERVING: 103 calories, fat 2g, protein 19g, carbohydrate 0g, fiber 0g

Freezer Friendly: Allow the chicken to cool completely before slicing. Spread the chicken slices in a single layer on a baking tray lined with parchment paper and freeze until solid. Store in a zip-top plastic bag in the freezer.

Make Plant Based: Swap the chicken breast for tempeh, tofu, seitan, or Gardein Chick'n Breasts. Use the same marinade for all but the Gardein product. Cook for just 3 to 4 minutes on each side, or until well browned.

Grilled Lemon Paprika Shrimp

For convenience, use peeled shrimp in this recipe; however, when grilling shrimp with a thicker sauce or marinade, the shells keep all of those yummy flavors close to the shrimp. If you don't have a grill basket, thread the shrimp onto bamboo skewers to keep them from falling through the grill grates.

YIELD: 4 (3-ounce) portions | PREP TIME: 5 minutes | COOK TIME: 5 minutes

1. Light a charcoal or gas grill, or preheat a grill pan. If you're using gas or a pan, you can wait to do this step until just before you're ready to cook.

2. Place the shrimp in a mixing bowl and drizzle with the olive oil. Toss gently to coat. Season with the paprika, lemon zest, sea salt, and pepper. Toss gently to coat.

3. Thread the shrimp onto two or three bamboo skewers (they do not need to be soaked).

4. Grill the shrimp for 2 to 3 minutes on each side until browned on the edges and opaque throughout.

1 pound peeled, deveined jumbo shrimp
1 teaspoon extra-virgin olive oil
1 teaspoon smoked paprika
1 teaspoon lemon zest
½ teaspoon sea salt
freshly ground black pepper

NUTRITION PER SERVING: 94 calories, fat 2g, protein 18g, carbohydrate 0g, fiber 0g

Kale Salad with Grilled Chicken and Citrus Vinaigrette

Spicy sambal, tangy kumquats, and savory grilled chicken make this kale salad irresistible. The black rice works surprisingly well in the salad because each of the grains stays intact.

YIELD: 4 servings | PREP TIME: 10 minutes | COOK TIME: 0 minutes

2 cups Steamed Black Rice (page 77)

12 ounces Grilled Chicken Breast (page 78), sliced

12 cups roughly chopped kale

2½ tablespoons canola oil

¼ cup lime juice

1¼ teaspoons sugar, honey, or maple syrup

½ teaspoon sea salt

½ to 1 teaspoon sambal chile paste

4 kumquats, thinly sliced with peel, or zest of one orange

¼ cup minced green onions

1. Place the black rice, chicken breast, and kale into the covered container, keeping them side by side but not mixing.

2. Combine the canola oil, lime juice, sugar, sea salt, chile paste, kumquats or orange zest, and green onions in a small jar. Cover the jar and place it into the meal prep container.

3. Cover and refrigerate for up to 4 days until ready to serve.

4. To serve: Pour the dressing over the kale and use clean hands to massage the dressing into the kale until it wilts and darkens. This will take about 30 seconds. Stir the kale and chicken into the salad.

NUTRITION PER SERVING: 400 calories, fat 13g, protein 31g, carbohydrate 40g, fiber 4g

Chicken Fajita Bowl with Avocado Lime Dressing

Sometimes meal-prepped dishes have too few carbs and lack in flavor. Not this one! Roasted sweet potatoes, peppers, and onions are rich in complex carbs and fiber. They're delicious with a tangy avocado lime dressing and grilled chicken.

YIELD: **4 servings** | PREP TIME: **5 minutes** | COOK TIME: **0 minutes**

1 recipe Roasted Fajita Vegetables (page 75)

2 small avocados

2 limes, juiced

12 ounces grilled chicken breast (page 78), sliced

sea salt

Freezer Friendly: Place the entire dish into the freezer. Allow to defrost overnight before serving. Remove the avocado dressing and warm the chicken and vegetables in a microwave if desired.

Note: If you're not going to eat the dish within a day of preparation, consider waiting to make the avocado lime dressing until you're ready to serve.

1. Place the sweet potatoes and the onion and pepper mixture into a covered container, keeping them side by side but not mixing. Top with slices of chicken.

2. In a small jar, mash the avocado, lime juice, and a pinch of sea salt. Cover and tuck into the larger covered container.

3. Cover and store in the refrigerator for up to 3 days until ready to serve.

4. To serve: Remove the avocado dressing and warm the chicken and vegetables in a microwave if desired. Alternately, serve the dish chilled. Drizzle the avocado dressing over the chicken and vegetables before serving.

NUTRITION PER SERVING: 487 calories, fat 14g, protein 32g, carbohydrate 59g, fiber 12g

Black Rice Pilaf with Grilled Shrimp and Peppers

This simple rice pilaf is bursting with flavor from sweet red bell peppers, smoked paprika, and a tangy lemon paprika vinaigrette.

YIELD: 4 servings | PREP TIME: 5 minutes | COOK TIME: 0 minutes

1 lemon, juiced

2 teaspoons smoked paprika, optional

1 tablespoon extra-virgin olive oil

½ teaspoon sea salt

2 cups Steamed Black Rice (page 77)

¼ cup minced green onions

12 ounces Grilled Lemon Paprika Shrimp (page 79)

2 red bell peppers, thinly sliced

½ cup roughly chopped toasted cashews

1. Whisk the lemon juice, smoked paprika, if using, olive oil, and salt in a small jar. Pour this over the black rice and add the green onions.

2. Divide the mixture between serving dishes and top with the shrimp, peppers, and cashews.

3. Cover and store in the refrigerator for up to 3 days until ready to serve.

NUTRITION PER SERVING: 404 calories, fat 16g, protein 26g, carbohydrate 45g, fiber 4g

Variation Tip: For a heftier meal, serve this as a filling for quesadillas. Use a total of 8 medium tortillas and add ½ cup refried black beans and 2 tablespoons shredded mozzarella cheese per serving.

Mango, Tofu, and Snap Pea "Stir-Fry"

I have been making some rendition of this dish since I worked for an Asian newspaper in Portland and reviewed a Thai cookbook featuring a similar recipe. Unlike the original, I opt for a fraction of the oil and swap the fish sauce for readily available soy sauce. I also use tofu instead of chicken thighs.

YIELD: **4 servings** | PREP TIME: **5 minutes** | COOK TIME: **0 minutes**

1. Place the snap peas, mango, and tofu into the meal prep container.

2. Whisk the lime juice, sesame oil, soy sauce, and chile paste in a separate jar. Pour over the entire dish.

3. Cover and refrigerate for up to 4 days until ready to serve.

NUTRITION PER SERVING: 503 calories, fat 17g, protein 30g, carbohydrate 59g, fiber 8.5g

4 cups halved snap peas, strings removed

2 cups diced fresh or frozen mango

1 recipe Crispy Roasted Tofu (page 76)

2 cups Steamed Black Rice (page 77)

2 limes, juiced

2 teaspoons toasted sesame oil

¼ cup low-sodium, gluten-free soy sauce

2 teaspoons sambal chile paste, or pinch of crushed red pepper

Spicy Salad Roll in a Bowl

This recipe began as a salad roll with spicy peanut dipping sauce. But I wanted more food and less fuss, so I added sliced chicken breast and lettuce and it became a delicious lunch that is filling and mess free.

YIELD: 4 servings | PREP TIME: 5 minutes | COOK TIME: 0 minutes

8 cups roughly chopped lettuce

2 cups shredded cabbage

2 medium avocados, thinly sliced

4 radishes, thinly sliced

12 ounces Grilled Chicken Breast (page 78), sliced

½ cup Soy Ginger Peanut Sauce (page 104) or store-bought peanut sauce

1. Divide the lettuce, cabbage, avocados, and radishes between meal-prep containers.

2. Top with the sliced chicken. Drizzle the dressing over the chicken or store it separately in individual containers to add just before serving.

NUTRITION PER SERVING: 343 calories, fat 22g, protein 25g, carbohydrate 16g, fiber 9g

WEEK 6

■ ■ ■ ■

SHEET PAN SAUSAGE AND VEGETABLE BAKE

The sheet pan does most of the work this week roasting up a big platter of sausage and vegetables. The foundation recipe is naturally very low in carbs, so if you follow a low-carb diet, there's no need to add to it—simply dish up one serving into a meal-prep container and you're good to go. Alternately, make the menu recipes and serve over quinoa, mix into a savory frittata, and add to a delicious soup. One quick and easy vegetarian recipe and a chicken dinner round out the week.

FOUNDATION RECIPES

Poached Chicken

Sheet Pan Sausage and Veggie Bake

Quinoa

Additional Prep Day Tasks

Chop vegetables for Thai Red Curry

MAIN MEALS

Roasted Vegetables and Sausage over Quinoa

Italian Sausage and Orzo Soup

Quinoa with Black Beans and Avocado

Frittata with Roasted Vegetables and Sausage

Thai Red Curry Chicken Noodle Bowl

WEEK 6 SHOPPING LIST

PANTRY STAPLES

- ☐ Extra-virgin olive oil
- ☐ Canola oil
- ☐ Low-sodium soy sauce
- ☐ Sea salt
- ☐ Freshly ground pepper
- ☐ Smoked paprika

MEAT, POULTRY, AND FISH

- ☐ 4 bone-in chicken thighs, about 6 ounces each
- ☐ 2 pounds Italian pork sausage (mild or hot)

DAIRY AND EGGS

- ☐ 1 dozen eggs (8 needed)

PACKAGED AND BULK FOODS

- ☐ 2 cups quinoa
- ☐ 8 ounces orzo pasta
- ☐ 4 ounces wide rice noodles

CANNED GOODS

- ☐ 1 (15-ounce) can plum tomatoes
- ☐ 1 (4-ounce) jar Thai red curry paste
- ☐ 2 quarts chicken broth
- ☐ 1 (14-ounce) can full-fat coconut milk
- ☐ 1 (15-ounce) can black beans

PRODUCE

- ☐ 1 bunch flat-leaf parsley
- ☐ 1 bunch fresh basil
- ☐ 1 bunch cilantro
- ☐ 1 head garlic
- ☐ 2 bunches broccoli
- ☐ 2 medium zucchini
- ☐ 2 medium yellow onions
- ☐ 3 large bell peppers (red, green, and yellow)
- ☐ 3 limes
- ☐ 1 bunch green onions
- ☐ 1 pint grape tomatoes
- ☐ 2 medium avocados
- ☐ 1 serrano pepper

SAVVY SHORTCUTS

- Buy chicken broth.
- Buy a rotisserie chicken.
- Buy precut vegetables.

Poached Chicken

Talk about killing two birds with one stone, or in this case one pot. This method produces flavorful cooked chicken meat and a savory chicken broth. In this recipe, I call for bone-in chicken thighs. You can use the same method for boneless pieces of chicken or a whole chicken; simply adjust the cooking times accordingly. Boneless meat cooks in about 15 minutes. A whole chicken will cook in about 45 to 60 minutes.

YIELD: 4 (4-ounce) servings cooked chicken meat, 12 (1-cup) servings (3 quarts) chicken broth | PREP TIME: 5 minutes | COOK TIME: 55 minutes

1. Place the chicken, water, parsley, and garlic into a large pot. Add the salt and bring to a simmer over medium heat. Simmer until the chicken is cooked through, about 25 minutes.

2. Remove the chicken from the pot and carefully remove the meat from the bones.

3. Return the chicken bones to the pot and simmer for another 30 minutes. Strain the broth through a fine-mesh sieve. Discard the bones, herbs, and garlic. Store the broth in a covered container in the refrigerator for up to one week.

4 bone-in, skinless chicken thighs, about 6 ounces each

3½ quarts water

1 sprig fresh parsley

1 smashed garlic clove

1 teaspoon sea salt

CHICKEN NUTRITION PER SERVING: 206 calories, fat 10g, protein 28g, carbohydrate 0g, fiber 0 g

BROTH NUTRITION PER SERVING: 10 calories, fat 1g, protein 1g, carbohydrate 0g, fiber 0g

Sheet Pan Sausage and Veggie Bake

For many years, I cut sausage into pieces before roasting. While this does infuse the vegetables with flavor, if you roast the sausages whole, the casing keeps all of the flavor in the meat and keeps it moist and tender. It's really up to you.

YIELD: 12 servings | PREP TIME: 10 minutes | COOK TIME: 40 minutes

1 bunch broccoli, cut into florets

2 medium zucchini, cut into 1-inch pieces

1 medium onion, sliced into 8 wedges

2 large bell peppers, cored and sliced into spears

2 pounds mild or hot Italian pork sausage, optionally cut into 1-inch pieces

1 tablespoon canola oil

sea salt

freshly ground pepper

1. Preheat the oven to 375°F. Line a rimmed baking sheet with parchment paper.

2. Spread the broccoli, zucchini, onion, peppers, and sausage onto the prepared pan. Drizzle with the canola oil and season generously with salt and pepper.

3. Roast for 30 minutes. Stir the ingredients and return to the oven for another 10 minutes until gently browned.

NUTRITION PER SERVING: 325 calories, fat 26g, protein 17g, carbohydrate 7g, fiber 3g

Freezer Friendly: Allow the cooked tray to cool completely then transfer to the freezer. Freeze until solid and then divide into storage containers, either zip-top plastic bags or meal-prep containers.

Make Plant-Based: To make this recipe vegan, use a plant-based sausage such as Field Roast or Beyond Meat Italian Sausage (for a gluten-free option) in place of the Italian sausage.

Quinoa

This ancient grain isn't a grain at all. It's actually a seed and, as such, is a good source of protein. It contains nearly twice the amount of protein as brown rice and slightly fewer carbs. Some people rinse quinoa first to remove the saponins, a somewhat astringent and bitter-tasting residue. But I usually skip the step because I don't notice a major difference in taste in the cooked quinoa.

YIELD: 8 (¾-cup) servings | PREP TIME: 2 minutes | COOK TIME: 20 minutes

1. Place the quinoa and water into a medium pot and season with salt.

2. Bring to a simmer over high heat, then reduce the heat to low, cover, and cook until all of the liquid has been absorbed, about 15 minutes.

3. Leave the quinoa in the pot to steam for another 5 minutes.

Freezer Friendly: Allow the quinoa to cool completely and then measure into zip-top plastic bags and freeze.

NUTRITION PER SERVING: 160 calories, fat 3g, protein 6g, carbohydrate 29g, fiber 3g

2 cups quinoa

4 cups water

½ teaspoon sea salt

Roasted Vegetables and Sausage Over Quinoa

I hesitate to even call this a recipe because it is so easy and makes the most out of your 1-hour of prep on the weekend.

YIELD: **4** servings | PREP TIME: **5** minutes | COOK TIME: **5** minutes

1. Warm the ingredients separately. The sausage and vegetables can be heated in a skillet over medium heat for 5 minutes. The quinoa can be warmed in the microwave or on the stove in a covered container or pot with 1 tablespoon of water.

2. Divide the warmed ingredients between serving dishes.

3. Alternately, divide the prepared ingredients into individual meal-prep containers and refrigerate until ready to serve. Warm for 1 to 2 minutes in the microwave.

NUTRITION PER SERVING: 485 calories, fat 29g, protein 23g, carbohydrate 36g, fiber 6g

1/3 of the Sheet Pan Sausage and Veggie Bake (page 90)

3 cups cooked Quinoa (page 92)

Italian Sausage and Orzo Soup

Fresh herbs, pungent garlic, and savory chicken broth breathe new life into the roasted vegetables and sausage in this comforting soup. The orzo pasta is optional, and a low-carb option with nutrition facts is included if you prefer.

YIELD: **4 servings** | PREP TIME: **5 minutes** | COOK TIME: **10 minutes**

1 teaspoon extra-virgin olive oil

2 garlic cloves, crushed

¼ cup minced fresh parsley

1 (15-ounce) can plum tomatoes, hand crushed

2 quarts (8 cups) Chicken Broth (page 89)

8 ounces orzo pasta

1/3 of Sheet Pan Sausage and Veggie Bake (page 90)

¼ cup roughly chopped fresh basil

1. Heat the olive oil in a large pot over medium heat. Add the garlic and cook for 30 seconds, until fragrant. Add the parsley, tomatoes, and chicken broth, and bring to a simmer.

2. Add the orzo pasta and cook for 8 minutes.

3. Add the sausage and vegetables and cook for another 1 to 2 minutes, or until heated through. Stir in the fresh basil.

NUTRITION PER SERVING: 583 calories, fat 29g, protein 26g, carbohydrate 59g, fiber 5g

Make Gluten Free: Use gluten-free orzo pasta or another gluten-free pasta, such as elbow macaroni

Low-Carb Option: For fewer carbs, omit the orzo pasta.

LOW-CARB NUTRITION PER SERVING: 383 calories, fat 28g, protein 19g, carbohydrate 17g, fiber 3g

Quinoa with Black Beans and Avocado

This simple chilled quinoa pilaf has been a staple in my house since my friend Christi shared it with me nearly a decade ago. It's surprisingly flavorful, winning over even the avowed carnivores. It works well for grab-and-go lunches or a chilled weeknight summer supper. This can be made up to one day in advance, but it is best to keep the ingredients separate if you want to store it for longer periods of time; the avocado spoils quickly once cut.

YIELD: 4 servings | PREP TIME: 10 minutes | COOK TIME: 0 minutes

1. Place the quinoa, black beans, grape tomatoes, cilantro, avocados, and green onions in a large serving bowl.

2. In a separate container, whisk the lime zest and juice, olive oil, serrano pepper, paprika, and garlic. Season with salt and pepper to taste.

3. Drizzle the dressing over the salad and toss gently to mix.

NUTRITION PER SERVING: 413 calories, fat 17g, protein 14g, carbohydrate 54g, fiber 14g

High-Protein Option: Swap the black beans for 16 ounces of cooked chicken breast.

HIGH-PROTEIN NUTRITION PER SERVING: 451 calories, fat 19g, protein 33g, carbohydrate 37g, fiber 7g

3 cups cooked Quinoa (page 92)

1 (15-ounce) can of black beans, rinsed and drained

1 pint grape tomatoes, halved

½ bunch cilantro, roughly chopped

2 medium avocados, diced

3 green onions, sliced on a bias

2 limes, zest and juice

2 tablespoons extra-virgin olive oil

1 to 4 teaspoons minced serrano pepper

1 teaspoon smoked paprika

1 garlic clove, minced

sea salt

freshly ground black pepper

Frittata with Roasted Vegetables and Sausage ⊘ ⊘ ⊘

I love having eggs for dinner because they're so easy to cook and are ready in minutes. They also make delicious leftovers. In fact, the classic Spanish tapas tortilla is typically served at room temperature.

YIELD: 4 servings | PREP TIME: 5 minutes | COOK TIME: 10 minutes

1 tablespoon canola oil

⅓ Sheet Pan Sausage and Veggie Bake (page 90)

¼ cup minced fresh parsley

8 eggs, whisked

sea salt

freshly ground pepper

1. Preheat the oven to 400°F.

2. Heat a large cast iron skillet or other oven-proof pan over medium-high heat. Warm the canola oil and then add the sausage and vegetables. Cook until just heated through.

3. Add the parsley and eggs to the pan and season with salt and pepper. Continue cooking on the stovetop for 3 minutes.

4. Transfer the pan to the oven and cook for another 5 minutes, or until heated through. Slice into wedges to serve.

NUTRITION PER SERVING: 499 calories, fat 39g, protein 30g, carbohydrate 8g, fiber 3g

Thai Red Curry Chicken Noodle Bowl

Although you technically can make your own curry paste, it's much easier to purchase bottled curry paste than to hunt down fresh lemongrass, kaffir lime leaves, and galangal. The intoxicating aromas and flavors of those authentic ingredients permeate the broth in this filling noodle bowl. Add the full three tablespoons of curry paste for the most flavor and spice.

YIELD: 4 servings | PREP TIME: 5 minutes, plus 10 minutes inactive time | COOK TIME: 10 minutes

1. Place the rice noodles in a heat-proof bowl and cover with very hot water for 10 minutes, while you cook the vegetables. Drain and set aside.

2. In a large pot, heat the canola oil over medium-high heat. Sauté the onion for 2 minutes, until it just begins to pick up some color.

3. Add the bell pepper, broccoli, curry paste, coconut milk, chicken broth, and soy sauce.

4. Bring to a simmer, cover, and cook until the vegetables are just tender, about 8 minutes.

5. Stir in the chicken and lime juice. Season with salt and pepper.

6. Divide the noodles between serving bowls and top with the coconut curry vegetables and chicken.

NUTRITION PER SERVING: 546 calories, fat 31g, protein 35g, carbohydrate 35g, fiber 4g

Low-Carb Option: Omit the rice noodles.

LOW-CARB NUTRITION PER SERVING: 454 calories, fat 30g, protein 33g, carbohydrate 12g, fiber 4g

4 ounces wide rice noodles

1 teaspoon canola oil

1 yellow onion, halved and thinly sliced

1 red bell pepper, cored and thinly sliced

1 head broccoli, cut into florets

2 to 3 tablespoons Thai red curry paste

1 (14-ounce) can full-fat coconut milk

1 cup Chicken Broth (page 89)

¼ cup low-sodium soy sauce

16 ounces Poached Chicken (page 89)

1 lime, juiced

sea salt

freshly ground pepper

WEEK 7

■ ■ ■ ■

PLANT POWERED

Over the years, my personal philosophy of eating has shifted from one centered on animal protein to one based on plants. Hence, many of the meals I cook for my own family are vegetarian or vegan. This chapter is all about showing you how delicious and filling plant-based meals can be! Warning, you might just love how you feel so much that you start finding more ways to incorporate plants into your diet. This week's primary protein is lentils. Stay with me here! They have 18 grams of protein per cup and are a good stand-in for ground beef in Lentil Shepherd's Pie and Lentil Sloppy Joes. They're also delicious just being themselves, as in the chilled Everything Goes Lentil Salad.

FOUNDATION RECIPES

Lentils

Mashed Potatoes

Ginger Red Wine Vinaigrette

Tangy Barbecue Sauce

Soy Ginger Peanut Sauce

Additional Prep Day Tasks

Cook noodles and green beans
for Soy Ginger Noodle Bowl

Assemble Lentil Shepherd's Pie

Chop vegetables for Everything
Goes Lentil Salad

MAIN MEALS

Lentil Shepherd's Pie

Everything Goes Lentil Salad

Lentil Sloppy Joes with
Apple Cabbage Slaw

BBQ Tempeh with Mashed
Potatoes and Collards

Soy Ginger Noodle Bowls with
Mango and Green Beans

WEEK 7 SHOPPING LIST

PANTRY STAPLES

- ☐ Apple cider vinegar
- ☐ Olive oil
- ☐ Canola oil
- ☐ Low-sodium soy sauce
- ☐ Toasted sesame oil
- ☐ Garlic powder
- ☐ Onion powder
- ☐ Smoked paprika
- ☐ Ground cumin
- ☐ Brown sugar, maple syrup, or agave
- ☐ All-purpose flour or gluten-free flour blend
- ☐ Mayonnaise (vegan if desired)
- ☐ Natural peanut butter or almond butter
- ☐ Sea salt
- ☐ Freshly ground pepper

MEAT, POULTRY, AND FISH

- ☐ 2 (8-ounce) packages tempeh

DAIRY AND EGGS

- ☐ 1 quart unsweetened almond milk
- ☐ 1 (8- to 14-ounce container) non-dairy butter, such as Earth Balance Buttery Spread

FROZEN

- ☐ 1 (8-ounce) package frozen peas

PACKAGED AND BULK FOODS

- ☐ 4 cups green lentils
- ☐ 2/3 cup walnuts
- ☐ 1/4 cup roughly chopped toasted peanuts or cashews
- ☐ 4 whole-grain hamburger buns
- ☐ 10 ounces whole-grain pasta

CANNED GOODS

- ☐ 1 (6-ounce) can tomato paste
- ☐ Jar of sriracha or sambal chili paste
- ☐ 1/2 cup dry red wine, optional
- ☐ 1 cup vegetable broth
- ☐ 1 (15-ounce) can chickpeas
- ☐ liquid smoke (optional)

PRODUCE

- ☐ 2½ pounds russet potatoes, peeled and quartered
- ☐ 1 head garlic
- ☐ 1 (2-inch) piece ginger
- ☐ 2 shallots
- ☐ 1 small yellow onion

- ☐ 2 stalks celery
- ☐ 2 medium carrots
- ☐ 1 lemon
- ☐ 1 lime
- ☐ 8 ounces mushrooms
- ☐ 1 bunch fresh thyme
- ☐ 2 cups cauliflower florets

- ☐ 1 bunch fresh kale
- ☐ 1 bunch fresh spinach
- ☐ 1 small red cabbage
- ☐ 2 Granny Smith apples
- ☐ 1 red onion
- ☐ 1 red bell pepper, cored and sliced

- ☐ 1 bunch collard greens
- ☐ 2 cups green beans
- ☐ 1 large carrot
- ☐ 1 small bell pepper
- ☐ 1 medium mango
- ☐ 1 bunch green onions
- ☐ 1 bunch fresh cilantro

SAVVY SHORTCUTS

- Buy prepared barbecue sauce.
- Buy prepared peanut sauce.
- Use boxed mashed potatoes.
- Use precut onions, carrots, and celery (mirepoix) for Lentil Shepherd's Pie.

Lentils

From a cooking perspective, lentils are the gateway legume. They are so easy to prepare and require no soaking, unlike other legumes. I didn't even know canned lentils were a thing until I saw them suggested as an option in a recipe. (Please don't go that route!) Just buy them in a bag or in bulk, grab a pot of water, and you're good to go. When you rinse and sort the lentils, you're looking for any errant twigs, rocks, or other debris.

YIELD: 10 (1-cup) servings | PREP TIME: 5 minutes | COOK TIME: 20 minutes

1. Place the lentils in a large pot and cover with the water. Bring to a vigorous boil over high heat.

2. Reduce the heat to low, so the water is at the barest simmer. Cover and cook for 20 minutes, or until the lentils are soft but not mushy.

3. Stir in the sea salt. Allow to cool and then store in a covered container in the refrigerator.

4 cups green lentils, rinsed and sorted

8 cups water

1 teaspoon sea salt

NUTRITION PER SERVING: 230 calories, fat 1g, protein 18g, carbohydrate 40g, fiber 16g

Freezer Friendly: Divide the cooled lentils between zip-top plastic bags. Lay each bag on its side and press all of the air from the bag. Seal and label. Freeze in a flat layer.

Mashed Potatoes

Russet potatoes are starchier than Yukon Gold potatoes, but either will work in this recipe. If you have a potato ricer, you can save time by not peeling the potatoes before cooking. The ricer will also give you a more uniform consistency.

YIELD: 10 (½-cup) servings | PREP TIME: 10 minutes | COOK TIME: 20 minutes

2½ pounds russet potatoes, peeled, quartered

1 teaspoon sea salt

½ cup unsweetened almond milk

⅓ cup non-dairy butter, such as Earth Balance Buttery Spread

1. Place the potatoes in a large pot and cover with water. Bring to a vigorous boil and cook for 15 minutes, or until the potatoes are very tender.

2. Run the potatoes through a potato ricer or place them in a bowl and use a potato masher.

3. Stir in the salt, almond milk, and non-dairy butter.

NUTRITION PER SERVING: 130 calories, fat 6g, protein 2g, carbohydrate 18g, fiber 3g

Ginger Red Wine Vinaigrette

This versatile vinaigrette is the perfect complement to the Everything Goes Lentil Salad (page 106); or, make a double batch and toss it with mixed greens for a healthy side salad.

YIELD: 1 cup, or 8 (2-tablespoon) servings | PREP TIME: 5 minutes | COOK TIME: 0 minutes

½ cup red wine vinegar

3 tablespoons olive oil

2 teaspoons minced garlic

1 teaspoon minced ginger

2 tablespoons maple syrup

2 shallots, minced

sea salt

freshly ground pepper

Combine all of the ingredients in a glass jar, cover, and shake to mix. Store in the refrigerator.

NUTRITION PER SERVING: 61 calories, fat 4g, protein 0g, carbohydrate 5g, fiber 0g

Tangy Barbecue Sauce

Most commercially available barbecue sauces have as much sugar as cake frosting does—not exactly what you want to smother over your healthy, plant-based dinner. This version gets its flavor from apple cider vinegar, tomato paste, and a generous dose of spices. A hint of brown sugar or maple syrup keeps it pleasantly sweet.

YIELD: 1 cup, or 8 (2-tablespoon) servings | PREP TIME: 2 minutes | COOK TIME: 25 minutes

1. Place the apple cider vinegar, tomato paste, garlic powder, onion powder, smoked paprika, cumin, and sea salt in a medium sauce pan. Bring to a simmer and cook for 25 minutes, until reduced to about 1 cup.

2. Stir in the brown sugar, adding more to taste.

3. Store in a covered container in the refrigerator for up to 1 week.

NUTRITION PER SERVING: 26 calories, fat 0g, protein 1g, carbohydrate 8g, fiber 1g

1 cup apple cider vinegar

½ cup tomato paste

½ teaspoon garlic powder

½ teaspoon onion powder

1 teaspoon smoked paprika

¼ teaspoon ground cumin

¼ teaspoon sea salt

2 tablespoons brown sugar or maple syrup

Soy Ginger Peanut Sauce

The sweet, spicy, and savory flavors in this dressing will have you licking your plate!

YIELD: ½ cup sauce, or 4 (2-tablespoon) servings | PREP TIME: 5 minutes | COOK TIME: 0 minutes

¼ cup low-sodium and/
or gluten-free soy sauce

1 teaspoon toasted sesame oil

2 tablespoons natural peanut
butter or almond butter

1 teaspoon brown sugar,
maple syrup, or agave

2 tablespoons lime juice

1 tablespoon minced ginger

1 teaspoon minced garlic

1 teaspoon chile sauce, such
as sambal or sriracha

Combine all of the ingredients in a small jar. Cover tightly
and shake to mix.

NUTRITION PER SERVING: 73 calories, fat 6g, protein 2g,
carbohydrate 4g, fiber 1g

Lentil Shepherd's Pie

To save a dish, prepare this meal in a cast iron skillet. Allow it to cool before covering because cast iron holds onto heat and can keep foods warm long after it has left the stove. This flavorful, plant-based recipe is adapted from one of my favorite vegan cookbooks, **Vegan Cooking for Carnivores** *by Roberto Martin. Include steps 1 through 6 in your weekend prep.*

YIELD: 4 servings | PREP TIME: 10 minutes | COOK TIME: 33 to 43 minutes

1. Preheat the oven to 375°F.

2. Heat the canola oil in a large skillet over medium-high heat. Cook the onion, celery, and carrots for 5 minutes, until the vegetables soften slightly and begin to pick up some color. Push them to the sides of the pan.

3. Add the mushrooms to the pan and cook for 2 minutes. Add the thyme and garlic, and cook until just fragrant, about 30 seconds.

4. Pour the red wine into the pan, if using, and cook for 2 minutes, or until mostly evaporated.

5. Stir the flour into the pan and cook for 1 minute, or until it is mostly dissolved. Add the vegetable broth and lentils, and simmer for 2 to 3 minutes, or until thickened. Stir in the frozen peas.

6. Remove the pan from the heat and season to taste with salt and pepper.

7. Transfer the lentil and vegetable mixture to a second baking dish, if using. Spread the prepared mashed potatoes over the dish, cover tightly with foil, and bake for 20 minutes. Alternately, refrigerate until ready to bake, and bake for 30 minutes.

1 tablespoon canola oil

1 cup diced onion

1 cup diced celery

1 cup diced carrots

1 cup roughly chopped mushrooms

1 tablespoon minced fresh thyme

1 teaspoon minced garlic

½ cup dry red wine, optional

2 tablespoons all-purpose flour or gluten-free flour blend

1 cup vegetable broth

4 cups cooked Lentils (page 101)

½ cup frozen peas

3 cups prepared Mashed Potatoes (page 102)

sea salt

freshly ground pepper

NUTRITION PER SERVING: 519 calories, fat 13g, protein 24g, carbohydrate 80g, fiber 23g

Freezer Friendly: Cover the shepherd's pie tightly with plastic wrap then cover with aluminum foil and freeze. Remove the plastic wrap and replace the foil before baking at 375°F for 1½ hours.

Everything Goes Lentil Salad

The title of this recipe would be much longer if it reflected the myriad yummy plants tucked into it—"Lentil, chickpea, cauliflower, and kale salad with apples, walnuts, and spinach, in a tangy soy ginger dressing." Wow, that's a mouthful! Like other plant-based meals, you'll find this one helps you easily meet your daily fiber requirements. Chop the cauliflower, kale, spinach, cabbage, and apple during your weekend prep day.

YIELD: 4 servings | PREP TIME: 5 minutes | COOK TIME: 0 minutes

2 cups cooked chickpeas, rinsed and drained

2 cups cauliflower florets

2 cups shredded fresh kale

2 cups fresh spinach

1 cup shredded cabbage

1 small apple, cored and diced

3 cups cooked Lentils (page 101)

⅓ cup roughly chopped walnuts

½ cup Ginger Red Wine Vinaigrette (page 102)

Divide the chickpeas, cauliflower, kale, spinach, cabbage, apple, and lentils into individual serving dishes. Keep the walnuts and vinaigrette in separate containers until ready to serve. Enjoy chilled or at room temperature.

NUTRITION PER SERVING: 530 calories, fat 15g, protein 27g, carbohydrate 80g, fiber 25g

Lentil Sloppy Joes with Apple Cabbage Slaw

These tangy, messy sandwiches are a childhood favorite with a healthy twist. Instead of ground beef, they're packed with healthy vegetables and lentils. Don't worry, they're still loaded with flavor from the Tangy Barbecue Sauce (page 103) and cumin-scented apple cabbage coleslaw.

YIELD: 4 servings | PREP TIME: 10 minutes | COOK TIME: 7 minutes

1 tablespoon canola oil

1 red onion, halved and sliced, divided

1 red bell pepper, cored and sliced

3 cups Lentils (page 101)

½ cup Tangy Barbecue Sauce (page 103)

2 tablespoons mayonnaise (use vegan if desired)

1 teaspoon ground cumin

1 tablespoon lemon juice

2 cups shredded cabbage

1 small Granny Smith apple, thinly sliced

4 whole-grain hamburger buns, toasted if desired

sea salt

freshly ground pepper

1. Heat the canola oil in a large skillet over medium-high heat. Sauté half of the onion and bell pepper for 5 minutes, until the vegetables have picked up some color and are beginning to soften.

2. Add the lentils and barbecue sauce and bring to a simmer for 2 minutes. Remove the pan from the heat and season to taste with salt and pepper.

3. While the vegetables cook, mix the mayonnaise, cumin, and lemon juice in a separate bowl. Season with salt and pepper. Add the cabbage, remaining sliced onion, and apple to the bowl, and mix to coat.

4. Place half of each hamburger bun on a serving plate and top with a generous scoop of the lentil mixture and some of the coleslaw. Top with the remaining burger bun. Enjoy immediately.

NUTRITION PER SERVING: 482 calories, fat 11g, protein 20g, carbohydrate 72g, fiber 15g

Note: To completely prepare this meal ahead of time, store the ingredients in separate containers: the barbecue lentil mixture, the sliced cabbage, onion, and apple, the dressing, and the buns.

Make Vegan and Egg-Free: Use a vegan mayonnaise.

BBQ Tempeh with Mashed Potatoes and Collards

This yummy plant-based plate delivers the satisfying flavors of the deep South. Most recipes for Southern-style collard greens call for stewing the greens for a long time. This version takes a different approach with a quick sauté so the leafy green is brightly colored and retains most of its nutritional value. Less time, more nutrients.

YIELD: **4 servings** | PREP TIME: **5 minutes** | COOK TIME: **6 minutes**

1. Heat 1 tablespoon of the canola oil in a large skillet over medium-high heat. Pan fry the tempeh for about 2 minutes on each side until gently browned. Remove the pan from the heat and add the barbecue sauce. This can be done ahead of time.

2. In a separate pan, heat the remaining ½ tablespoon of canola oil in a large, deep skillet over medium-high heat. Sauté the collard greens until they're bright green, about 1½ minutes. Add the garlic and cook for another 30 seconds. Add the liquid smoke and apple cider vinegar and season to taste with salt and pepper.

3. Divide the mashed potatoes between serving plates. Top with the BBQ tempeh and serve the collard greens on the side.

NUTRITION PER SERVING: **332 calories, fat 18g, protein 15g, carbohydrate 32g, fiber 6g**

Ingredient Tip: The liquid smoke in the collard greens adds a nice smoky element, reminiscent of bacon, but you can use smoked paprika if you prefer not to buy another ingredient. Note, a little goes a long way, so be careful as you measure!

1½ tablespoons canola oil, divided

1 (8-ounce) package tempeh, halved horizontally, then cut into 2-inch pieces

½ cup Tangy Barbecue Sauce (page 103)

1 bunch collard greens, cut into thin ribbons

1 teaspoon minced garlic

½ teaspoon liquid smoke, optional

2 teaspoons Apple Cider Vinegar

2 cups Mashed Potatoes (page 102), warmed

Soy Ginger Noodle Bowls with Mango and Green Beans

The sweet, spicy, and savory flavors in this colorful noodle bowl are healthy and addicting. Soy sauce, lime juice, fresh ginger, and garlic permeate whole-grain noodles studded with mango, julienned carrots, and green beans. It is the perfect one-dish meal. Complete steps 1 through 3 on your weekend prep day. If you have the time, chop the carrot, bell pepper, and mango as well.

YIELD: **4 servings** | PREP TIME: **10 minutes** | COOK TIME: **10 minutes**

10 ounces whole-grain pasta, cooked

2 cups halved green beans, about 8 ounces, blanched

2 teaspoons canola oil

1 (8-ounce) package tempeh, cut into 1 x 2-inch rectangles ¼-inch thick

½ cup Soy Ginger Peanut Sauce (page 104)

1 large carrot, julienned

1 small red bell pepper, sliced

1 medium mango, diced

¼ cup roughly chopped toasted peanuts or cashews

1 green onion, green parts only, thinly sliced on a bias

½ cup minced fresh cilantro

1. Bring a large pot of salted water to a boil. Cook the pasta according to the package instructions.

2. During the last 2 minutes of the pasta cooking, add the green beans.

3. Drain the pasta and green beans and rinse briefly under cool running water.

4. While the pasta cooks, heat the canola oil in a large skillet over medium-high heat. Sear the tempeh for about 2 minutes on each side, until well browned.

5. Place the cooked pasta in a container with a lid and pour the peanut sauce over it.

6. Add the carrot, bell pepper, mango, tempeh, cashews, green onion, and cilantro. Toss gently to mix. Serve at room temperature or cover and store in the refrigerator for up to 3 days.

NUTRITION PER SERVING: 570 calories, fat 19g, protein 21g, carbohydrate 82g, fiber 9g

Make Gluten-Free: Use brown rice pasta and gluten-free soy sauce in the peanut sauce.

▪ ▪ ▪ ▪
BREAKFAST

Whether you work from home, send kids racing out the door to school, or enjoy a long commute by train, chances are, breakfast needs to be fast, healthy, and convenient. This chapter provides recipes that you can make ahead of time and then serve or prepare in just two minutes or less. For the most important meal of the day, that's two minutes well spent!

Quinoa, Fruit, and Lime Pilaf

Quinoa for breakfast? Sure! If other grains such as oats and corn grits make sense, so does quinoa. Technically a seed, not a grain, quinoa is a rich source of protein, fiber, and complex carbohydrates. Use whatever fresh fruit is in season in your area to make this yummy chilled breakfast salad, such as grapes, strawberries, blueberries, raspberries, or mango. To make it seem more like breakfast cereal, you can also pour a half cup of almond milk over each serving when you're ready to eat it.

YIELD: 4 servings | PREP TIME: 5 minutes | COOK TIME: 20 minutes

1 cup quinoa, rinsed and drained

2 cups water

pinch sea salt

6 cups diced fresh fruit

4 mint leaves, thinly sliced

2 tablespoons fresh lime juice

¼ cup roughly chopped toasted almonds

1. Place the quinoa in a small pot, cover with water, and add a pinch of sea salt. Bring the water to a simmer, cover, and cook over low heat for 15 to 20 minutes, or until the quinoa has absorbed all of the water. Fluff with a fork and allow to cool completely.

2. Toss the quinoa with the fruit, mint, and lime juice. Divide between four serving containers and top with the slivered almonds.

NUTRITION PER SERVING: 261 calories, fat 6g, protein 8g, carbohydrate 46g, fiber 8g

Ingredient Tip: Fruits with greater antioxidant amounts will not brown as quickly after being cut. The fruits listed are a good choice, but bananas and apples will oxidize after being cut.

Frozen Smoothie Packs

I could drink a smoothie for breakfast every day for the rest of my life and be completely content. Let's face it—even when they're chock-full of good-for-you-ingredients like frozen bananas, almond milk, and a scoop of protein powder, most smoothies feel like a delicious milkshake for breakfast. Don't worry though, these shakes pack a hefty nutritional punch. Many ingredients can be found already frozen, such as strawberries, pineapple, and mango. For these, simply divide between the freezer bags and proceed with the recipe as written.

YIELD: 4 servings | PREP TIME: 2 minutes, plus freezing time | COOK TIME: 0 minutes

Creamy Chocolate Banana Smoothie

4 frozen bananas, sliced in ½-inch-thick pieces

4 tablespoons almond butter or tahini

4 scoops of your favorite chocolate protein powder

4 cups unsweetened almond milk

1. To freeze the banana, spread it in slices onto a rimmed baking sheet lined with parchment paper. Freeze until solid, about 1 hour. Place into a zip-top plastic bag, remove most of the air from the bag, and seal tightly until ready to use.

2. To blend, place all of the ingredients into a blender and puree until completely smooth, scraping down the sides as needed.

NUTRITION PER SERVING: 353 calories, fat 13g, protein 31g, carbohydrate 37g, fiber 8g

Strawberry Power Greens

1. To freeze the banana slices, power greens, strawberries (if fresh), and avocado, spread them onto a rimmed baking sheet lined with parchment paper. Freeze until solid, about 1 hour. Divide between four zip-top plastic bags, remove most of the air from the bags, and seal tightly until ready to use.

2. To blend, place all of the ingredients into a blender and puree until completely smooth, scraping down the sides as needed.

NUTRITION PER SERVING: 244 calories, fat 14g, protein 4g, carbohydrate 28g, fiber 9g

2 frozen bananas, sliced in ½-inch thick pieces

8 cups frozen power greens blend, such as baby spinach, chard, and kale

2 cups fresh or frozen strawberries

1 large frozen avocado, diced

¼ cup pepitas (raw pumpkin seeds)

4 to 6 cups water

Tropical Twist Smoothie

1. To freeze the banana slices, mangos, and pineapple, spread them onto a rimmed baking sheet lined with parchment paper. Freeze until solid, about 1 hour. Place into a zip-top plastic bag, remove most of the air from the bag, and seal tightly until ready to use.

2. To blend, place all of the ingredients into a blender and puree until completely smooth, scraping down the sides as needed.

NUTRITION PER SERVING: 338 calories, fat 6g, protein 23g, carbohydrate 49g, fiber 5g

2 frozen bananas, sliced in ½-inch thick pieces

2 cups diced frozen mangos

2 cups diced frozen pineapple

4 cups light coconut milk or almond milk

4 scoops strawberry or vanilla protein powder

Overnight Raspberry Chia Pudding

Make these simple chia puddings in a half-pint mason jar. This makes it easy to just add the liquid ingredients, shake vigorously, and set in the refrigerator overnight to set.

YIELD: 4 servings | PREP TIME: 5 minutes | COOK TIME: 0 minutes

¾ cup (12 tablespoons) chia seeds

2 cups unsweetened vanilla soy milk

2 tablespoons maple syrup

2 cups fresh or frozen raspberries

Divide all of the ingredients between individual serving jars with lids. Shake gently to mix. Refrigerate overnight.

NUTRITION PER SERVING: 281 calories, fat 11g, protein 13g, carbohydrate 33g, fiber 20g

Raw Fruit and Nut Bars

I began making my own version of the popular LARABAR about seven years ago and love how I can customize them to my flavor preferences and make a huge batch for a fraction of the cost of the packaged version. Here are my favorite flavor combinations. They're a yummy grab-and-go breakfast or healthy snack.

YIELD: 8 bars | PREP TIME: 5 minutes | COOK TIME: 0 minutes

1. Place the almonds, walnuts, and sea salt into a food processor and pulse until finely ground.

2. Add the pitted dates and vanilla extract to the blender and blend until the dates are evenly distributed and the mixture holds together when shaped into a ball.

3. Add the ingredients from your favorite variation and pulse until just integrated.

4. Dump the mixture out onto a clean cutting board and shape into a rectangle about 1-inch thick. Cut the rectangle into 8 bars and wrap each one individually in parchment paper or plastic wrap. Refrigerate until ready to serve for up to 1 week.

NUTRITION PER SERVING (FOR BASE RECIPE): 213 calories, fat 14g, protein 5g, carbohydrate 21g, fiber 4g

¾ cup almonds

¾ cup walnuts

¼ teaspoon sea salt

1 cup pitted dates

½ teaspoon vanilla extract

Cherry Chocolate Chunk

½ cup dried cherries

½ cup dark chocolate chips

Brownie Batter

½ cup dark chocolate chips

2 tablespoons unsweetened cocoa powder

Coconut Lime

¼ cup unsweetened coconut

1 teaspoon lime zest

1 teaspoon lime juice

Health Monster Muffins

These tasty muffins hide a powerful secret—they're chock-full of healthy vegetables, fruit, and nuts. Okay, it's not exactly a secret, but they taste so good even the kids and vegetable averse will love them. They're lightly sweetened with applesauce and maple syrup or brown sugar.

YIELD: 12 muffins | PREP TIME: 10 minutes | COOK TIME: 20 to 23 minutes

1½ cups whole-wheat pastry flour or whole-grain, gluten-free flour blend

1½ teaspoons baking powder

1 teaspoon baking soda

1 teaspoon ground cinnamon

½ teaspoon sea salt

¾ cup applesauce

3 tablespoons maple syrup or brown sugar

1/3 cup canola oil

2 carrots, shredded

1 small zucchini, shredded

½ cup raisins

¼ cup finely chopped walnuts

1. Preheat the oven to 350°F. Line a standard 12-cup muffin tin with parchment paper liners.

2. Whisk the flour, baking powder, baking soda, cinnamon, and salt in a medium mixing bowl. Stir in the applesauce, maple syrup, and canola oil.

3. Fold in the carrots, zucchini, raisins, and walnuts.

4. Divide the batter between the prepared muffin cups. Bake for 20 to 23 minutes, or until the muffins are gently browned. Allow to cool before serving or storing in an airtight container. They will keep longer if stored in the refrigerator.

NUTRITION PER MUFFIN: 166 calories, fat 8g, protein 3g, carbohydrate 25g, fiber 3g

Freezer Friendly: The muffins can be frozen and stored in a zip-top plastic bag. Try to remove as much air as you can from the bag before sealing and freezing.

Sundried Tomato and Parmesan Egg Muffin Cups

When it comes to savory breakfasts, it's nice to find one that is ready when you are. Usually it involves standing at the stove to prepare a meal. And, while eggs cook instantly, egg muffin cups are ready even quicker and you don't have to dirty any dishes.

YIELD: 6 (2-muffin) servings | PREP TIME: 5 minutes | COOK TIME: 15 minutes

1. Preheat the oven to 375°F.

2. Blend the eggs and sea salt in a blender.

3. Coat a 12-cup muffin pan with the butter or line with parchment paper liners and pour the egg batter into each cup.

4. Divide the spinach, sundried tomatoes, green onion, and Parmesan between muffin cups.

5. Bake for 15 minutes. Allow to cool completely before storing in a covered container in the refrigerator.

NUTRITION PER SERVING: 183 calories, fat 12g, protein 14g, carbohydrate 5g, fiber 1g

Freezer Friendly: Yes, you can toss these into the freezer! Just freeze individually, then place in a zip-top plastic bag, remove as much air as possible, label, and freeze until ready to serve. Microwave for 2 minutes, or until heated through.

10 eggs

1 teaspoon sea salt

1 tablespoon butter or olive oil, optional

1½ cups shredded spinach

½ cup sliced sundried tomatoes

½ cup minced green onion

½ cup shredded Parmesan cheese

Sausage, Onion, and Basil Egg Muffin Cups

Savory sausage and fragrant basil permeate these delicious egg muffin cups.

YIELD: 6 (2-muffin) servings | PREP TIME: 5 minutes | COOK TIME: 15 minutes

10 eggs

1 teaspoon sea salt

1 tablespoon butter or olive oil, optional

12 ounces cooked, crumbled sausage

½ cup minced red onion

¼ cup minced fresh basil

1. Preheat the oven to 375°F.

2. Blend the eggs and sea salt in a blender.

3. Coat a 12-cup muffin pan with the butter or line with parchment paper liners and pour the egg batter into each cup.

4. Divide the sausage, onion, and basil between muffin cups.

5. Bake for 15 minutes. Allow to cool completely before storing in a covered container in the refrigerator.

NUTRITION PER SERVING: 281 calories, fat 21g, protein 18g, carbohydrate 2g, fiber 0g